AF695504

DEEPENING TRADE AND TRANSPORT FACILITATION POLICY ANALYSIS OF BORDER CROSSING POINTS

EXPANDING THE CAREC CORRIDOR PERFORMANCE MEASUREMENT AND MONITORING FRAMEWORK

JULY 2025

ASIAN DEVELOPMENT BANK

6 ADB Avenue, Mandaluyong City, 1550 Metro Manila, Philippines
Tel +63 2 8632 4444; Fax +63 2 8636 2444
www.adb.org

ISBN 978-92-9277-380-9 (print); 978-92-9277-381-6 (PDF); 978-92-9277-382-3 (ebook)
Publication Stock No. TCS250302-2
DOI: http://dx.doi.org/10.22617/TCS250302-2

Notes:
In this publication, "$" refers to United States dollars.
ADB recognizes "China" as the People's Republic of China.
ADB placed its regular assistance to Afghanistan on hold effective 15 August 2021.

Cover design by Eric Mercado.

Contents

Tables, Figures, and Boxes

Tables

Figures

Boxes

Foreword

The Central Asia Regional Economic Cooperation (CAREC) Program has played a key role in advancing regional cooperation and integration among its 11 member countries. As the CAREC region seeks to strengthen trade and investment linkages, the need for better connectivity, efficient institutional coordination, and trade facilitation has become increasingly important. Despite abundant natural resources and the strategic location linking major markets, CAREC countries continue to face significant challenges in harnessing their full trade and economic potential. These include limited export diversification, low foreign direct investment inflows, and ongoing challenges at border crossing points (BCPs).

The Asian Development Bank (ADB) has been a long-standing partner of the CAREC Program, supporting its efforts to foster a region that is connected, competitive, and inclusive. ADB has helped catalyze investments in transport infrastructure and supported trade policy reforms and institutional capacity building. To support these initiatives, ADB introduced the Corridor Performance Measurement and Monitoring (CPMM) framework to evaluate the efficiency of BCPs and transport corridors, and to provide empirical evidence such as time and cost measures to guide policy and investment decisions.

This report aims to build upon the current CPMM framework by developing a holistic and practical methodology to assess the quality of trade and transport facilitation at major BCPs across the CAREC region. Aligned with the CAREC Integrated Trade Agenda 2030, the study introduces the Cross-Border Trade and Transport Facilitation Index (CBTTFI)—a tool designed to provide deeper, BCP-level insights into the operational, institutional, and regulatory barriers affecting cross-border trade.

Based on analysis of data from structured and extensive surveys, the report offers a detailed evaluation of selected BCPs in Azerbaijan, Georgia, Pakistan, Turkmenistan, and Uzbekistan. The findings present specific challenges and opportunities related to customs efficiency, interagency coordination, transit infrastructure, and regulatory harmonization. Importantly, the study translates these insights into practical recommendations for customs modernization, enhanced risk management, infrastructure development, and harmonized transport standards.

By equipping policymakers and development partners with a more comprehensive diagnostic toolkit, the CBTTFI offers a timely contribution to evidence-based policy formulation and project design. It supports ongoing efforts to reduce trade costs, enhance corridor performance, and help policymakers in their endeavors to realize the CAREC vision of seamless connectivity and shared prosperity.

ADB remains committed to working closely with CAREC countries to implement the recommendations of this study and deepen regional integration. We hope this report serves as a valuable resource for governments, customs authorities, traders and transport service providers, and development practitioners.

Albert Park
Chief Economist and Director General
Economic Research and Development Impact Department
Asian Development Bank

Acknowledgments

This publication was prepared by the Regional Cooperation and Integration Division (ERCI) of the Economic Research and Development Impact Department (ERDI) of the Asian Development Bank (ADB), with strong support from the Regional Cooperation and Integration Unit (CWRC) of ADB's Central and West Asia Department. The overall production of the publication was supported by ADB's Technical Assistance Support Fund 6668: Support for Forward-Looking Trade Facilitation Measures in Asia and the Pacific.

Jong Woo Kang, director of ERCI, ADB provided overall direction and supervision for the report. Kijin Kim, senior economist of ERCI, led the study project from conceptualization through research and report drafting. Aleli Rosario and Carol Ongchangco supported the report as both reviewers and coordinators. Shubham Gupta, ADB consultant, led the Deloitte team that contributed to the drafting of the report. The other members include Nishant Jain, Vardham Jain, and Priyavadhani S.

The publication benefited significantly from the valuable insights and guidance of Zulfia Khamitovna Karimova, as well as the CAREC Corridor Performance Monitoring and Measurement (CPMM) team, including Julius Santos, Max Ee, Andy Sze, and Camille Isles. The study team appreciates their seamless collaboration throughout the report development process from brainstorming, planning, data collection from public and private sector stakeholders, and to review. The report also benefited from the reviews provided by ADB's East Asia Department (Dorothea Ramizo) and the Climate Change and Sustainable Development Department (Wilhelmina T. Paz).

The feedback and strong support from Albert Park, Chief Economist and Director General of ERDI, is gratefully acknowledged.

The study team appreciates CWRC for facilitating opportunities to present initial findings of the study at the CAREC CPMM Methodology Workshop held in Tashkent, Uzbekistan in October 2024, and online consultation meeting with customs officials from CAREC member countries in December 2024. The insights and feedback received from the participants at these events guided the direction and enhanced the study.

Kijin Kim coordinated overall production, assisted by Aleli Rosario and Carol Ongchangco. Eric Van Zant edited the manuscript. Eric Mercado created the cover design. Joe Mark Ganaban typeset and did the layout. Maria Guia de Guzman proofread the report, while Lawrence Casiraya did the page proof checking, with support from Carol Ongchangco. Support for printing and publishing this report was provided by the Printing Services Unit of ADB's Corporate Services Department and by the publishing team of the Department of Communications and Knowledge Management.

Abbreviations

ADB	Asian Development Bank
AEO	authorized economic operator
ARCII	Asia-Pacific Regional Cooperation and Integration Index
BCP	border crossing point
CAREC	Central Asia Regional Economic Cooperation
CBTTFI	Cross-Border Trade and Transport Facilitation Index
PRC	People's Republic of China
CITA	CAREC Integrated Trade Agenda
CMR	Convention on the Contract for the International Carriage of Goods by Road
CPMM	corridor performance measurement and monitoring
FDI	foreign direct investment
ICT	information and communication technology
ITC	International Trade Centre
SPS	sanitary and phytosanitary
TBT	technical barriers to trade
TFI	trade facilitation indicator
TIR	Transports Internationaux Routiers (International Road Transport)
TTF	trade and transport facilitation
WTO	World Trade Organization

Highlights

The Central Asia Regional Economic Cooperation (CAREC) countries need to strengthen regional cooperation and accelerate economic diversification to address trade and investment challenges. CAREC's 11 member countries aim to foster economic development, regional integration, and poverty reduction. Yet this vast and diverse geographic region, although rich in natural resources—including oil, gas, and minerals—relies heavily on primary export of such commodities and is thus vulnerable to global commodity price fluctuations. And despite these endowments, the region's participation in global trade remains limited primarily due to geographic constraints, underdeveloped infrastructure, high trade costs, and limited export diversification. Foreign direct investment inflows also remain low, at around 1% of global foreign direct investment, with Kazakhstan and Mongolia attracting the highest shares, and others lagging, such as Pakistan and Tajikistan.

CAREC has prioritized trade and transport facilitation. To bridge economic disparities through regional cooperation, CAREC has mobilized over $51 billion in investments across 276 regional projects since 2001, with a strong focus on developing multimodal transportation networks, enhancing trade, enabling free movement of people and goods, and laying the groundwork for the development of economic corridors. Of these investments, transport has the biggest share, with about 67.4% or about $34.3 billion; while trade facilitation and trade policy accounts for 2.7% or about $1.4 billion. Kazakhstan received the largest share of total investment in transport (24.6%), followed by Uzbekistan (19%) and Azerbaijan (16.3%). The People's Republic of China (PRC) received the largest share under trade facilitation and trade policy (38.9%), followed by Pakistan (22.2%) and Mongolia (16.1%).

The Corridor Performance Measurement and Monitoring (CPMM) framework is helping data-driven trade and transport facilitation. Established in 2009, the CPMM is a critical empirical framework designed to assess the efficiency of goods movement across borders and along the six key CAREC transport corridors. By tracking time and cost to cross borders, total transport costs, and vehicle speeds, CPMM identifies operational bottlenecks both at and behind borders. Its time and cost-distance methodology enables insights into the performance of road and rail transport, offering a standardized, comparative lens for evaluating border crossing point (BCP) and corridor effectiveness.

The primary objective of this study is to expand the existing CPMM framework for evaluating the extent of trade and transport facilitation at BCPs. To attain the goal, the study focused on four thematic areas (i) customs procedures and formalities, (ii) customs coordination, (iii) transit cross-border support facilities, and (iv) transport regulations to develop a more comprehensive framework for evaluating trade and transport facilitation at BCPs in CAREC countries.

Methodology

The study employs a structured, six-workstream approach to evaluate trade and transport facilitation (Highlights Figure 1).

Highlights Figure 1: Workstream Approach of the Study

1. Identification of CAREC's trade and transport facilitation-based economic development priorities
2. Exploring coverage of existing trade and transport facilitation studies and frameworks
3. Assessment of CPMM's coverage of trade and transport-based economic priorities
4. Customizing assessment framework for holistic coverage of trade and transport themes
5. Data collation through primary and secondary research
6. Assessment of inputs and drafting of recommendations

CAREC = Central Asia Regional Economic Cooperation, CPMM = corridor performance measurement and monitoring.
Source: Study team's approach to the study.

Workstream 1: Identification of CAREC's trade and transport facilitation-based economic development priorities

A review of existing literature of CAREC Integrated Trade Agenda 2030 (CITA 2030), Rolling Strategic Action Plans, CITA 2030 Results Framework, focus areas for the Customs Cooperation Committee as well as the National Trade Readiness Assessment parameters applicable at BCP level was carried out. The strategic focus areas of all the frameworks were mapped to six broad trade and transport facilitation (TTF) thematic areas presented as shown in Highlights Figure 2.

Highlights Figure 2: Broad Trade and Transport Facilitation Thematic Areas

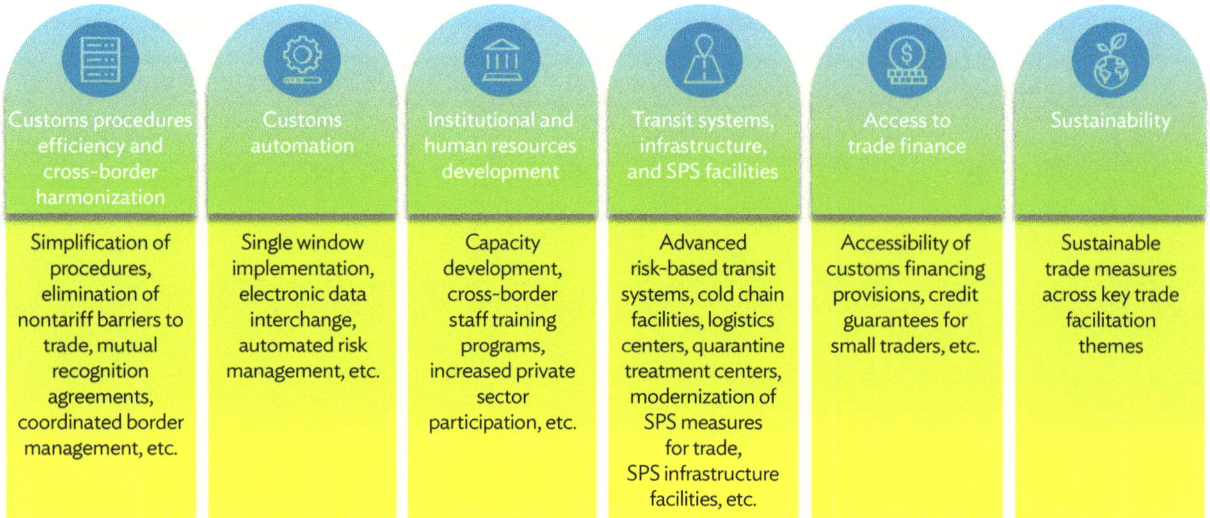

SPS = sanitary and phytosanitary.
Source: Study team's analysis based on existing literature.

Workstream 2: Exploring coverage of existing trade and transport facilitation studies and frameworks

The key themes of TTF identified as priorities for the CAREC region were compared with those outlined in the Sub-national Trade Readiness Assessment, as presented in the *Integrated Approach to Trade and Transport Facilitation* in 2022. The analysis found a strong alignment between the TTF themes identified in the 2022 study and CAREC's priority areas.

Workstream 3: Assessment of CPMM's coverage of trade and transport-based economic priorities

The performance of CAREC trade corridors is currently assessed through the CPMM framework, which provides valuable insights into trade efficiency along these routes. However, a cross-mapping of CPMM's coverage with the parameters of Sub-national Trade Readiness Assessment framework revealed that only 13 out of the 43 parameters of Sub-national Trade Readiness Assessment are covered by CPMM (directly/indirectly/partially). This highlights an opportunity to expand the existing CPMM exercise with additional tools that offer more granular, BCP-level insights.

Workstream 4: Customizing assessment framework for holistic coverage of trade and transport themes

To complement the existing CPMM framework, the Cross-Border Trade and Transport Facilitation Index (CBTTFI) has been proposed as a composite index for evaluating various trade and transport facilitation-related themes, based on survey-based responses from public and private sector stakeholders. The index covers 4 key themes and 10 underlying subthemes of trade and transport facilitation via road at BCPs (Highlights Figure 3).

Highlights Figure 3: Themes and Subthemes Under Cross-Border Trade and Transport Facilitation Index Framework

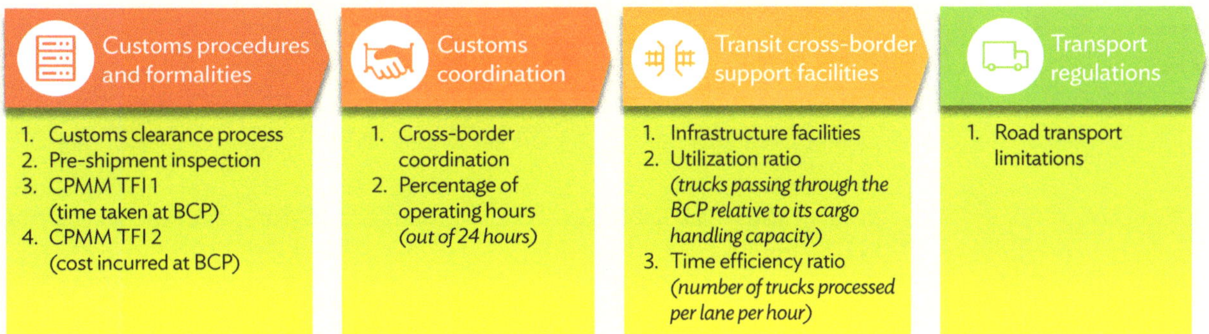

BCP = border crossing point, CPMM = corridor performance measurement and monitoring, TFI = trade facilitation indicator.
Source: Study team's proposal for the Cross-Border Trade and Transport Facilitation Index.

The study has also mapped CBTTFI questions with various CPMM activities. Based on this, the index enables policymakers to go beyond the CPMM data findings by uncovering the underlying reasons for high costs or delays across various activities identified in the CPMM analysis at specific BCPs.

Workstream 5: Data collation and analysis

For undertaking the assessment, six BCPs were selected, ensuring assessments could be performed for at least one pair of points, apart from facilitating intra-country and inter-country comparisons. Highlights Table 1 provides a snapshot of the scores for each BCP analyzed along with the mean score.

Highlights Table 1: Performance of Analyzed Border Crossing Points Under the Themes of Cross-Border Trade and Transport Facilitation Index

BCP Name	Country	Customs Procedures and Formalities (0.55)	Customs Coordination (0.15)	Transit Support Facilities (0.25)	Transport Regulations (0.05)	Total Weighted Average Score
Kirmizi Korpu	Azerbaijan	79%	77%	64%	0%	71%
Tsiteli Khidi	Georgia	69%	69%	62%	0%	64%
Serhetabat	Turkmenistan	57%	50%	67%	100%	60%
Farap	Turkmenistan	57%	77%	42%	100%	59%
Torkham	Pakistan	71%	88%	82%	50%	75%
Yallama	Uzbekistan	88%	85%	64%	0%	77%
Average		**70%**	**74%**	**64%**	**42%**	**68%**

BCP = border crossing point.
Note: The figures in parentheses represent weights selected for the analysis.
Source: Study team's calculation based on the Cross-Border Trade and Transport Facilitation Index survey.

Overall, the six BCPs score an average of 68% on the CBTTFI, with the highest average performance in *customs coordination* (74%), followed by *customs procedures and formalities* (70%), *transit support facilities* (64%), and *transport regulations* (42%).

By theme, Yallama in Uzbekistan scored highest in customs procedures and formalities (88%), while Torkham in Pakistan scored highest in customs coordination (88%) and support facilities (82%), and Turkmenistan's Serhetabat and Farap secured top scores in transport regulations theme (100%). Highlights Table 2 assesses selected border points along with their major characteristics.

Highlights Table 2: Evaluation of Border Crossing Points and Identified Gaps

Characteristics	Kirmizi Korpu (Azerbaijan)	Tsiteli Khidi (Georgia)	Serhetabat (Turkmenistan)	Farap (Turkmenistan)	Torkham (Pakistan)	Yallama (Uzbekistan)
Location	CAREC corridor 2, connecting Tbilisi, Georgia to Ganja, Azerbaijan	CAREC corridor 2, connecting Tbilisi, Georgia to Ganja, Azerbaijan	CAREC corridors 2 and 6, connecting Turkmenistan with Afghanistan	CAREC corridors 2 and 3, connecting the city of Farap, Turkmenistan with the city of Alat, Uzbekistan	CAREC corridors 5 and 6, connecting to Nangarhar province of Afghanistan	CAREC corridors 3 and 6 near the border with Kazakhstan
Maximum cargo handling capacity	30,000 trucks/ containers per month	29,550 trucks/ containers per month	5,700 trucks/ containers per month	24,000 trucks/ containers per month	72,000 trucks/ containers per month	30,000 trucks/ containers per month
No. of lanes exclusively for truck examination	6 lanes	5 lanes	1 lane	4 lanes	12 lanes	5 lanes
Operational hours	24 hours	24 hours	9 hours	24 hours	9 hours	24 hours

continued on next page

Highlights Table 2 *continued*

Characteristics	Kirmizi Korpu (Azerbaijan)	Tsiteli Khidi (Georgia)	Serhetabat (Turkmenistan)	Farap (Turkmenistan)	Torkham (Pakistan)	Yallama (Uzbekistan)
Customs procedures and formalities	**Score: 79%** **Features:** • Electronic processing of key documents • Deployment of most of the key ICT infrastructure • Prior intimation on documentation, testing and/or certification and inspection requirements • Pre-arrival clearance **Constraints:** • Cases of mandatory physical submission of original documents (passport/national ID card, commercial driver's license, liability and cargo insurance, etc.) which potentially increase the time taken for cargo vehicles to cross a BCPs along with added cost • Inadequate provisions for electronic application of customs refunds and e-CMR • Lack of provision to make advance fee payment for inspections • Computerized transit control systems, portable illegal drug identification systems with single window applications services are operational for only 50% of the time	**Score: 69%** **Features:** • Presence of ICT infrastructure • Prior intimation on documentation requirements before testing and/or certification • Advance fee payment for inspections • Pre-arrival clearance **Constraints:** • Mandatory physical submission of original documents (passport, visa, commercial driver's license, vehicle registration documents, SPS certificate and commercial invoice, etc.) which causes delay in the wait or queue time • Officials have overriding and/or discretionary powers to carry out physical inspections beyond findings of computerized risk assessment algorithms which account for 5%–10% inspection	**Score: 57%** **Features:** • Presence of major ICT infrastructure • Prior intimation of inspection requirements • Advance fee payment for inspections **Constraints:** • Mandatory physical submission of original documents for most of the cases • Lack of prior intimation on testing and/or certification requirements and pre-arrival clearance • Lack of prior intimation on testing and/or certification requirements • Time taken to cross BCP is the highest among the selected BCPs, at 5.5 hours for inbound traffic—nearly 4.8 hours greater than another BCP—Serhetabat in Turkmenistan	**Score: 57%** **Features:** • Presence of only major ICT infrastructure • Prior intimation of inspection requirements • Advance fee payment for inspections • Less than 5% physical inspection takes place based on the results from feedback of the assessment system **Constraints:** • Mandatory physical submission of original documents • Inadequate provision for digital payment of duties and taxes, electronic queue management systems, and electronic application for customs refunds • Time taken to cross the BCP is 30 hours for outbound traffic, while the cost incurred to cross the BCP is around $270	**Score: 71%** **Features:** • Electronic customs processing of documents • Presence of information and communication technology infrastructure • Prior intimation on testing and/or certification and inspection requirements • Pre-arrival clearance **Constraints:** • Officials have overriding and/or discretionary powers to carry out physical inspections beyond findings of computerized risk assessment algorithms which account for 5%–10% inspection • Mandatory physical submission of certain original documents	**Score: 88%** **Features:** • Electronic customs processing of documents • Presence of ICT infrastructure • Prior intimation on testing and certification requirements • Advance fee payment for inspections • Time taken to cross the BCP is 1.1 hours for inbound traffic, indicating faster processing, while the cost incurred to cross the BCP is also low at $15—the least cost among the selected BCPs **Constraints:** • Officials have overriding and/or discretionary powers to carry out physical inspections beyond the findings of computerized risk assessment algorithms which account for 5%–10% inspection

continued on next page

Highlights Table 2 *continued*

Characteristics	Kirmizi Korpu (Azerbaijan)	Tsiteli Khidi (Georgia)	Serhetabat (Turkmenistan)	Farap (Turkmenistan)	Torkham (Pakistan)	Yallama (Uzbekistan)
Customs coordination[a]	**Score: 77%** **Features:** • Provisions for interoperable information systems • Electronic data interchange between customs authorities of Azerbaijan and Georgia • Mutual recognition of major documents **Constraints:** • Inadequate synchronized clearance procedures with neighboring BCPs i.e., presently there is no coordinated border management—the border and customs controls are applied separately at each side of the BCP • Inspection and quality certificates are not mutually recognized	**Score: 69%** **Features:** • Electronic data interchange between customs authorities of Georgia and Azerbaijan • Mutual recognition of major documents **Constraints:** • Inadequate synchronized clearance procedures with neighboring BCPs i.e., presently there is no coordinated border management—the border and customs controls are applied separately at each side of the BCP • Mutual recognition of AEO certification and insurance documents is not present	**Score: 50%** **Features:** • Electronic data interchange between customs authorities • Mutual recognition of major documents **Constraints:** • Lack of synchronized clearance procedures with the neighboring BCPs and interoperable information systems between customs authorities • Mutual recognition of AEO certification and inspection and/or SPS certifications are not present • Low no. of operating hours of BCP (9 hours), namely other BCPs	**Score: 77%** **Features:** • Provisions for interoperable information systems • Synchronized clearance procedures • Electronic data interchange between customs authorities • Mutual recognition of major documents **Constraints:** • Mutual recognition of inspection and/or SPS certificates and AEO certification is not present	**Score: 88%** **Features:** • Provisions for interoperable information systems • Synchronized clearance procedures • Electronic data interchange between customs authorities • Mutual recognition of documents **Constraints:** • Low no. of operating hours of BCP (9 hours), namely other BCPs.	**Score: 85%** **Features:** • Provisions for interoperable information systems • Mutual recognition of requisite documents **Constraints:** • Synchronized clearance procedures and electronic data interchange between customs authorities are not present

continued on next page

Highlights Table 2 *continued*

Characteristics	Kirmizi Korpu (Azerbaijan)	Tsiteli Khidi (Georgia)	Serhetabat (Turkmenistan)	Farap (Turkmenistan)	Torkham (Pakistan)	Yallama (Uzbekistan)
Transit cross-border support facilities	**Score: 64%** **Features:** • Presence of major logistics support infrastructure **Constraints:** • Time efficiency index is quite low (4.7 trucks per lane per hour)—highest waiting and/or queuing time for inbound traffic as per CPMM data	**Score: 62%** **Features:** • Presence of major logistics support infrastructure **Constraints:** • Maintenance repair facilities for vehicles and cargo transloading terminals, available only in the vicinity of BCP, could be developed at the BCP • Significantly high utilization ratio where the BCP is operating beyond its maximum capacity	**Score: 67%** **Features:** • Presence of major logistics support infrastructure • High operational efficiency of cargo handling—utilization ratio for the BCP is 0.93 • Time efficiency index: 19.6 trucks per lane per hour—fastest among other BCPs **Constraints:** • Maintenance repair facilities for vehicles and cargo transloading terminals are available only in the vicinity of BCP	**Score: 42%** **Features:** • Presence of major logistics support infrastructure in the vicinity of BCP **Constraints:** • Maintenance repair facilities for vehicles, available in the vicinity of BCP, could be developed at BCP • Utilization ratio indicates underutilization • In spite of low utilization ratio, time efficiency index for the BCP is just 3 trucks per lane per hour	**Score: 82%** **Features:** • Presence of major logistics support infrastructure • High time efficiency index for the BCP—14.3 trucks per lane per hour, indicating that there is not much delay in the processing of customs cargo trucks	**Score: 64%** **Features:** • Presence of major logistics support infrastructure • Utilization ratio for the BCP is 0.89—indicating high operational efficiency
Transport regulations[b]	**Score: 0%** **Constraints:** Presence of weight and dimension limitations for cargo vehicles	**Score: 0%** **Constraints:** Presence of weight and dimension limitations for cargo vehicles	**Score: 100%** **Features:** No weight and dimension limitations for cargo vehicles	**Score: 100%** **Features:** No weight and dimension limitations for cargo vehicles	**Score: 50%** **Features:** No dimension limitations for cargo vehicles **Constraints:** Presence of weight limitation	**Score: 0%** **Constraints:** Presence of weight and dimension limitations for cargo vehicles

AEO = authorized economic operator, BCP = border crossing point, CPMM = corridor performance measurement and monitoring, e-CMR = electronic consignment note, ICT = information and communication technology, SPS = sanitary and phytosanitary.

[a] While some BCPs—such as Kirmizi Korpu, Farap, Torkham, and Yallama—have indicated the presence of interoperable systems based on survey responses from customs authorities, the actual extent of interoperability in terms of institutional readiness and on-ground implementation remains to be ascertained. The broader objective is to ensure the availability of truly interoperable systems at cross-border points, enabling alignment and seamless data exchange between the customs, transport, and trade facilitation systems of neighboring countries across the Central Asia Regional Economic Cooperation region.

[b] The analysis assumes the absence of weight and dimension restrictions at BCPs, owing to limited data availability, to be favorable. However, bilateral harmonization across BCP pairs is more critical, as mismatched restrictions can lead to delays or cargo rerouting. Harmonization needs to be prioritized wherever feasible.

Source: Study team's analysis based on the Cross-Border Trade and Transport Facilitation Index survey.

Workstream 6: Recommendations for selected border crossing points

Key recommendations for the border crossings have been categorized into five broad themes (Highlights Figure 4).

Highlights Figure 4: Broad Themes of Recommendations

Enhance customs efficiency and transparency	**Recommendation 1:** Digitalization of customs processes and inclusion of ICT infrastructure at the BCPs
Coordinate border-crossing operations	**Recommendation 2:** Synchronization of customs procedures at the BCPs
Efficient risk management operations	**Recommendation 3:** Prior intimation on testing/certification/inspection requirements before arrival at the BCPs and minimizing the overriding and/or discretionary decisions by customs officials for carrying out physical inspection beyond risk assessment
Expand cross-border transport and logistics infrastructure	**Recommendation 4:** Inclusion of cross-border support infrastructure at the BCPs
Harmonize transport and vehicle standards	**Recommendation 5:** Implement standard regulation for supporting border-crossing transit at the CAREC region

BCP = border crossing point, CAREC = Central Asia Regional Economic Cooperation, CPMM = corridor performance measurement and monitoring, ICT = information and communication technology, TFI = trade facilitation indicator.
Source: Study team's proposal for the Cross-Border Trade and Transport Facilitation Index.

Enhance customs efficiency and transparency

Improving customs efficiency through digitalization and information and communication technology (ICT) integration is essential for reducing delays, lowering transaction costs, and boosting trade across CAREC countries. Digitalization enables the automation of cross-border processes, allowing customs officials to submit and exchange documents electronically, such as declarations, invoices, certificates of origin, and cargo manifests. Enabling end-to-end digital document submission also enhances clearance speed, transparency, and recordkeeping, while physical copies of original documents may still be required for verification purposes. ICT integration at BCPs further improves efficiency and security through real-time monitoring and automated systems, including single window portals, customs management platforms, electronic payments with refund mechanisms, queue management tools, nonintrusive inspections, surveillance systems, and automated passport control. Highlights Figure 5 provides BCP recommendations to enhance customs efficiency and transparency.

Highlights Figure 5: Recommendations to Enhance Customs Efficiency and Transparency at Border Crossing Points

Kirmizi Korpu	Tsiteli Khidi	Serhetabat	Yallama	Farap	Torkham
• Provision for electronic processing of documents • Electronic application for customs refunds • Provisioning e-CMR for digital handling of transport documents • Focus on improving service level up time (single window portal, computerized transit control systems, and portable illegal drug identification)	• Provision for electronic processing of documents • Electronic application for customs refunds • Provisioning e-CMR facility • Development of customs mobile application for easy access	• Provision for electronic processing of documents • Digital payment of duties and/or taxes • Electronic application for customs refunds • Provisioning e-TIR and e-CMR for real-time data exchange • Electronic queue management system to reduce wait times	• Provision for electronic processing of customs declaration	• Provision for electronic processing of documents • Digital payment of duties and/or taxes • Electronic application for customs refunds • Provisioning e-TIR and e-CMR for real-time data exchange • Electronic queue management system to reduce wait times • Automated passport control systems to accelerate identity verification	• Focus on improving service level up time

e-CMR = electronic consignment note, e-TIR = electronic Transports Internationaux Routiers.
Source: Study team's suggestions based on the Cross-Border Trade and Transport Facilitation Index analysis.

Coordinate border-crossing operations

Effective coordination among customs authorities at BCPs is essential for reducing delays, minimizing costs, and promoting regional integration. CAREC countries can implement interoperable information systems with cross border electronic data interchange between customs authorities, synchronized clearance procedures, and mutual recognition of submitted documents. Customs agencies at border points can coordinate and conduct joint inspections, eliminating the need for multiple agencies to conduct separate inspections. Highlights Figure 6 provides recommendations to enhance coordination of border-crossing operations.

Highlights Figure 6: Recommendations to Enhance Coordination of Border-Crossing Operations

Kirmizi Korpu	Tsiteli Khidi	Serhetabat	Farap	Yallama
• Synchronized clearance procedures with neighboring BCPs • Mutual recognition of inspection and quality certifications	• Interoperable information systems for real-time data exchange • Synchronized clearance procedures with neighboring BCPs • Mutual recognition of AEO transporters and insurance documents	• Interoperable information systems between customs authorities • Synchronized clearance procedures with neighboring BCPs • Mutual recognition of inspection and/or SPS certification and AEO operators	• Mutual recognition of inspection and/or SPS certification and AEO operators	• Synchronized clearance procedures and electronic data interchange between customs authorities

AEO = authorized economic operator, BCP = border crossing point, SPS = sanitary and phytosanitary.
Source: Study team's suggestions based on the Cross-Border Trade and Transport Facilitation Index analysis.

Efficient risk management operations

The CAREC countries have adopted risk assessment in customs inspection, focusing on high-risk consignments based on algorithms and nonintrusive inspection scanning. However, certain constraints found in the survey include inadequate prior information on inspection requirements and customs officials have discretionary powers to conduct physical inspections apart from the risk assessment, which are potential factors for delays at border crossings. Implementing prior intimation systems for testing, certification, and inspection requirements for trucks before arrival at BCPs, ideally upon pre-arrival submission of documents, would facilitate transport.

Clear, standard operating procedures are also needed for customs officials for determining physical inspection. Customs officials overriding and/or discretionary powers to conduct physical inspections beyond the findings of risk assessment output could be minimized to enhance efficiency and streamlined process. Highlights Figure 7 showcases the recommendations for enhancing efficiency of risk management operations at BCPs.

Highlights Figure 7: Recommendations for Efficient Risk Management Operations at Border Crossing Points

Kirmizi Korpu	Tsiteli Khidi	Serhetabat	Torkham	Farap	Yallama
• Provision for advance fee payment for inspections	• Prior intimation of inspection requirements upon submission of pre-arrival information • Minimize the overriding and/or discretionary decisions by customs officials for physical inspection	• Prior intimation on testing and/or certification requirements • Provision for pre-arrival clearance process	• Minimize the overriding and/or discretionary decisions by customs officials for physical inspection	• Prior intimation on testing and/or certification requirements • Provision for pre-arrival clearance process	• Provision for pre-arrival clearance process • Minimize the overriding and/or discretionary decisions by customs officials for physical inspection

Source: Study team's suggestions based on the Cross-Border Trade and Transport Facilitation Index analysis.

Expand cross-border transport and logistics infrastructure

Cross-border transit support logistics infrastructure is a major requirement for faster border crossing and support to regional trade. Industrial infrastructure such as logistics hubs, dry ports, and warehouses at strategic locations can act as inland customs and logistics facilities for goods arriving by land. Product testing labs, quarantine treatment centers, electric generators, and communication facilities at borders can reduce congestion, speeding up cargo processing. Highlights Figure 8 showcases recommendations to expand cross-border transport and logistics infrastructure.

Highlights Figure 8: Recommendations to Expand Cross-Border Transport and Logistics Infrastructure

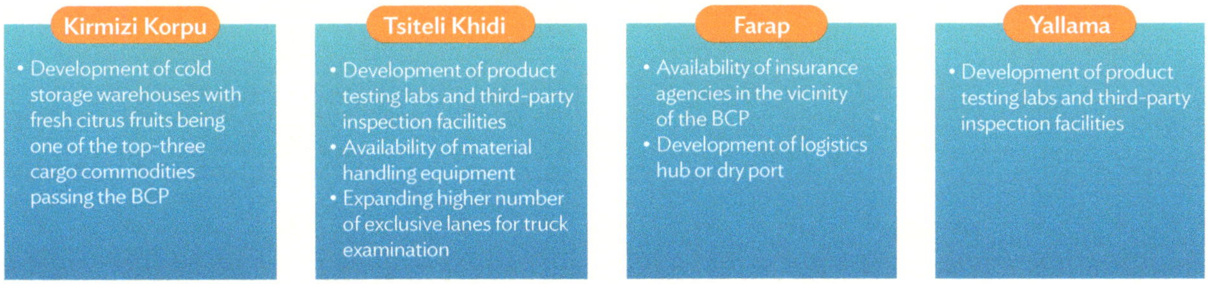

BCP = border crossing point.
Source: Study team's suggestions based on the Cross-Border Trade and Transport Facilitation Index analysis.

While Baku and Tbilisi offer strong logistics support to the Kirmizi Korpu–Tsiteli Khidi border crossing, a dedicated dry port or logistics hub at the border could enhance trade efficiency. However, given existing investments in regional infrastructure, a detailed feasibility study is recommended to assess demand, costs, and alignment with current facilities. Similarly, at the Farap BCP, a key gateway between Turkmenistan and Uzbekistan, a logistics hub or dry port may be beneficial. Yet, with existing infrastructure in nearby Turkmenabat, a feasibility study is essential to evaluate cargo volumes, existing capacity, connectivity to the transport network, and the cost–benefit of new development.

To enhance regional trade competitiveness, it is recommended to establish value-added processing centers near key border points such as Torkham, Pakistan, where recent infrastructure upgrades have improved trade efficiency. These centers can boost export value, reduce logistics costs, and create local jobs. Similar opportunities may be assessed at other strategic BCPs.

Harmonize transport and vehicle standards

Harmonizing transport and vehicle standards for CAREC border crossing is essential for trade facilitation, which requires strong political support. For this, CAREC member states need to prioritize transport and vehicle standards within their national agendas and regional cooperation frameworks.

CAREC countries may also work together to develop a regional agreement or memorandum of understanding that adopts common technical standards for vehicles, including safety requirements, emission standards, and dimension specifications. This includes harmonizing vehicle types, weight limits, axle configurations, and dimensions. This way of standardizing weight and dimension limits for trucks and containers eases customs processing of shipments.

1 Introduction

Trade and Investment Snapshot of CAREC Region

The 11 countries and institutions of the Central Asia Regional Economic Cooperation (CAREC) Program are working together to accelerate economic growth and poverty reduction. The member states—Afghanistan, Azerbaijan, the People's Republic of China (PRC), Georgia, Kazakhstan, the Kyrgyz Republic, Mongolia, Pakistan, Tajikistan, Turkmenistan, and Uzbekistan—span a vast and diverse area from the steppes and deserts of Central Asia to the mountainous regions of the Caucasus and South Asia.[1] Excluding the PRC, the region accounts for 5.5% of total land area in the world (~7 million square kilometers).[2]

Most of the CAREC countries are rich in natural resources. Azerbaijan and Kazakhstan are major oil and gas producers, while Mongolia, Turkmenistan, and Uzbekistan have significant mineral resources. The region's water resources are vital, especially where agriculture is significant, such as in countries like the Kyrgyz Republic and Tajikistan. However, overall economic growth in the region is primarily influenced by global commodity prices, especially for oil and gas. Efforts are ongoing to diversify economies away from reliance on natural resources toward manufacturing, agriculture, and services.

The CAREC countries share in world exports is low at 0.86% (excluding the PRC) as compared to regions such as Southeast Asia, which accounted for 7.67% and South Asia for 2.26% in 2023.[3] This situation is primarily due to geographical challenges such as landlocked countries, underdeveloped infrastructure, high trade costs in association with transit across borders, and lack of export diversification, which hinders the region's potential to compete effectively in the global market (Samad, Masood, and Ahmed 2023).

CAREC countries' often depend heavily on the export of commodities like crude oil and natural gas, making them vulnerable to price fluctuations. Further, trade numbers of the countries vary to a huge extent, as shown in Figure 1, which exhibits countries' trade figures for 2023. The CAREC region's exports of $202 billion in 2023 were dominated by Azerbaijan, Kazakhstan, and Pakistan, accounting for nearly 70% of total exports.

1 ADB placed its regular assistance to Afghanistan on hold effective 15 August 2021.
2 World Bank data. https://data.worldbank.org/indicator/AG.LND.TOTL.K2 (accessed 13 November 2024).
3 Study team's calculations based on ITC Trade Data. https://www.trademap.org/Index.aspx (accessed 6 March 2025).

Figure 1: Trade in CAREC Region, by Country

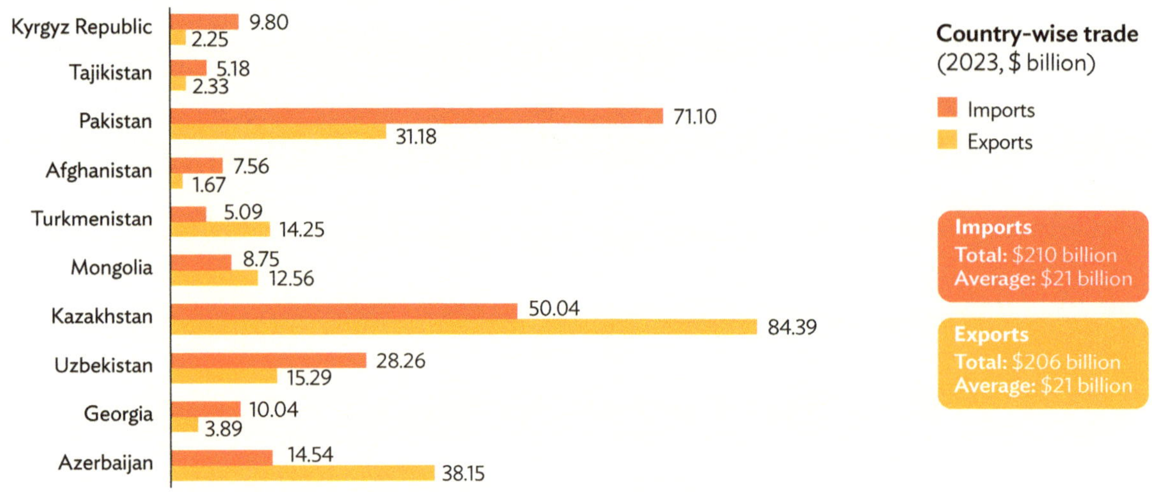

CAREC = Central Asia Regional Economic Cooperation.
Source: International Trade Centre Trade Map (accessed 6 March 2025).

CAREC region (excluding the PRC) attracted foreign direct investment (FDI) inflow of $13.3 billion in 2023, accounting for just ~1% of global FDI,[4] significantly lower than subregions like Southeast Asia (17%) and South Asia (3%).[5] Kazakhstan received nearly one-fourth of this inflow (Figure 2a), reflecting its openness to foreign investment and international integration (OECD 2023). However, as a share of gross domestic product, Mongolia stood out with FDI of 11%, far exceeding countries like Pakistan (0.5%) and Kazakhstan and Tajikistan (1.2% each) (Figure 2b).

The diverse economic profiles and varying levels of integration among CAREC member countries highlight the need for stronger regional cooperation to reduce economic disparities, enhance connectivity, and promote trade and investment for sustainable development.

4 UNCTAD FDI data. https://unctadstat.unctad.org/datacentre/dataviewer/US.FdiFlowsStock (accessed 6 March 2025).

5 Southeast Asia includes Brunei Darussalam, Cambodia, Indonesia, the Lao People's Democratic Republic, Malaysia, Myanmar, the Philippines, Singapore, Thailand, Timor-Leste, and Viet Nam; South Asia includes Afghanistan, Bangladesh, Bhutan, India, Maldives, Nepal, Pakistan, and Sri Lanka.

Figure 2: Share of Foreign Direct Investment in CAREC Region and Share of Foreign Direct Investment in Gross Domestic Product, by Country

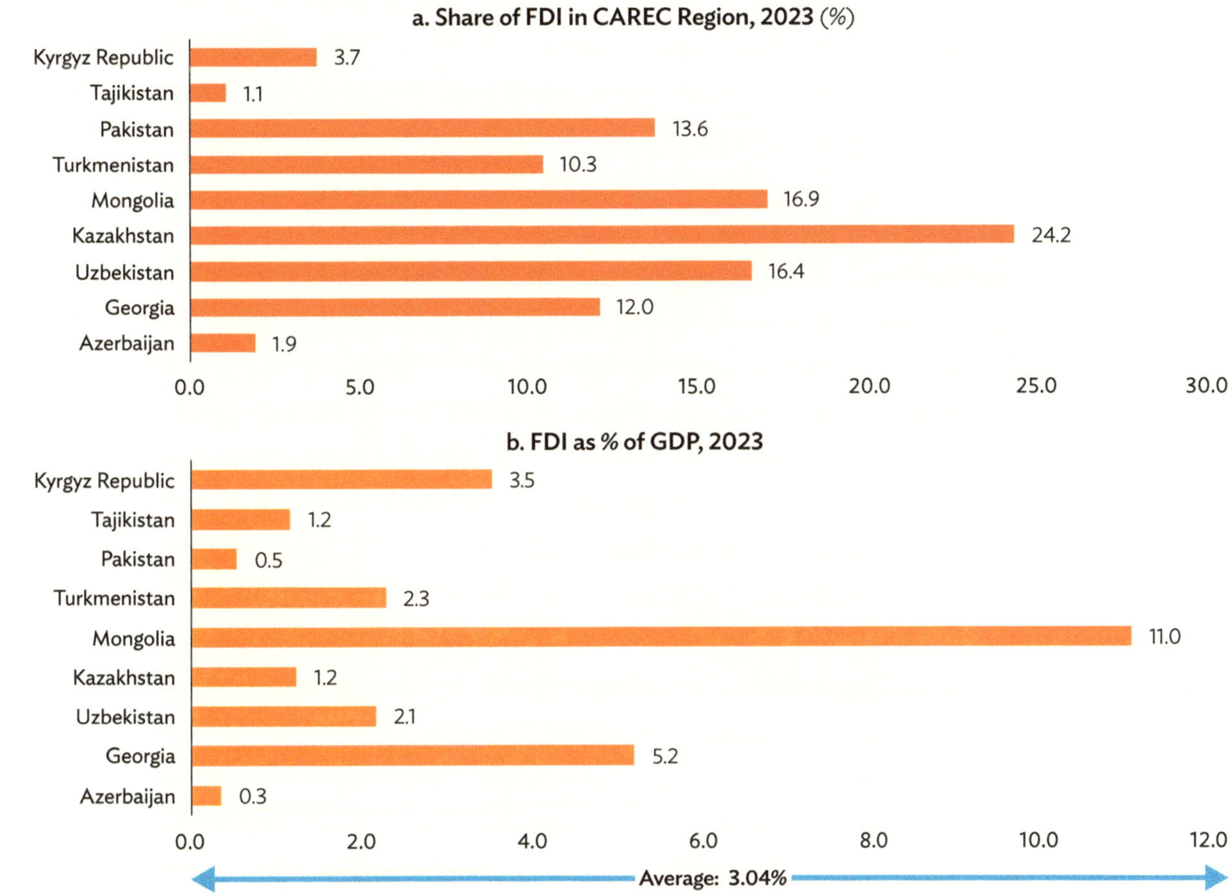

CAREC = Central Asia Regional Economic Cooperation, FDI = foreign direct investment, GDP = gross domestic product.
Source: United Nations Conference on Trade and Development. https://unctadstat.unctad.org/datacentre/dataviewer/US.FdiFlowsStock (accessed 6 March 2025).

Regional Cooperation in Trade and Transport Facilitation in CAREC

Investments in the CAREC region for regional cooperation and key projects undertaken

The CAREC Program fosters regional cooperation to promote economic integration, trade facilitation, and infrastructure development. The program promotes useful, outcome-driven regional projects and policy initiatives essential to the region's shared prosperity and long-term economic progress.

As of December 2023, CAREC had raised $51.02 billion in investments covering 276 regional projects since its founding in 2001.[6] Figure 3 presents CAREC investments by country for 2023. These investments have helped establish multimodal transportation networks, enhanced energy trade and security, allowed free movement of people and goods, and created the framework for the development of economic corridors.

Figure 3: CAREC Investment by Country

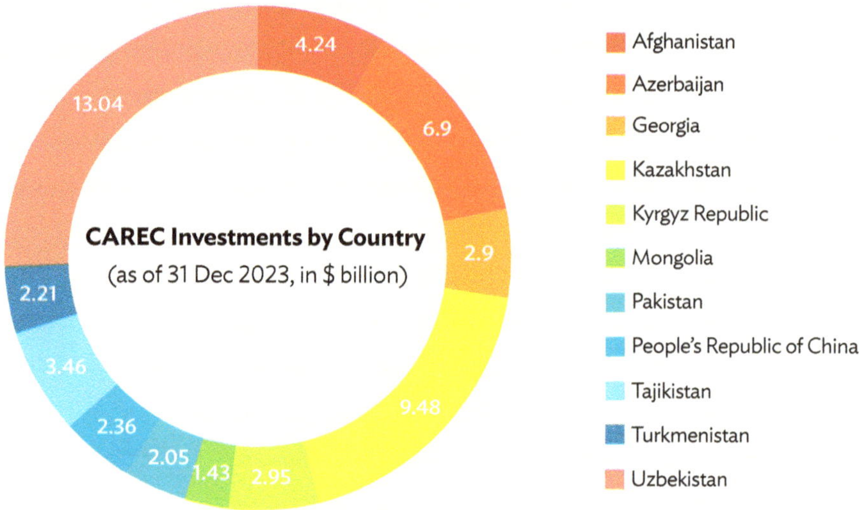

CAREC = Central Asia Regional Economic Cooperation.
Source: CAREC Project Portfolio. https://www.carecprogram.org/?page_id=13630 (accessed 13 November 2024).

The biggest share of investments has gone to transport, with about 67.5% or about $34.45 billion; while trade facilitation and trade-policy accounts for 2.7% or about $1.38 billion. Kazakhstan has received the largest share of total investments in transport (24.6%), followed by Uzbekistan (19%) and Azerbaijan (16.3%), and the PRC received the largest share under trade facilitation and trade policy (38.9%), followed by Pakistan (22.2%) and Mongolia (16.1%).[7]

Further, CAREC has identified and developed six major transport corridors crucial for enhancing regional connectivity. Investments are being made to upgrade road, rail, and port infrastructure along these corridors to improve efficiency and reduce transportation costs, promoting economic integration and access to markets. CAREC countries have also signed agreements to facilitate cross-border trade and transport.[8] These agreements aim to streamline border crossing procedures, reduce waiting times, and ensure smooth transit of goods and people.

6 CAREC investments were funded by CAREC governments (19.5%), by the Asian Development Bank (34.5%), and by other development partners (46%).

7 CAREC Project Portfolio. https://www.carecprogram.org/?page_id=13630 (accessed 13 November 2024).

8 Agreements such as the Cross-Border Transport Agreement signed by the Afghanistan, the Kyrgyz Republic, and Tajikistan under the CAREC Program; Pakistan–Uzbekistan Preferential Trade Agreement (signed and in-effect in 2023), Uzbekistan–Afghanistan Preferential Trade Agreement (signed and in-effect in 2024). https://www.carecprogram.org/?feature=first-cbta-signed-under-carec-december-2010; https://www.commerce.gov.pk/wp-content/uploads/2023/03/Uzbekistan-Pakistan-Preferential-Trade-Agreement-Rules-of-Origin-2023.pdf; https://trans.uz/en/news/preferential-trade-agreement-between-uzbekistan-and-afghanistan-to-enter-into-force-on-october-1.

Extent of regional cooperation on trade and investment integration among CAREC member countries

The Asia-Pacific Regional Cooperation and Integration Index (ARCII)[9] has been useful in evaluating the level of regional cooperation across regions, including CAREC countries.

Among the countries of CAREC region, overall, Mongolia scored highest (0.52) on the Regional Cooperation and Integration Index. The country also scored the highest (0.7) in the CAREC region under the *trade and investment integration* dimension of the ARCII, while Azerbaijan scored lowest, at 0.08. Figure 4 presents scores for the CAREC countries.

Figure 4: Score of CAREC Countries in Asia-Pacific Regional Cooperation and Integration Index and Its Trade and Investment Integration Dimension

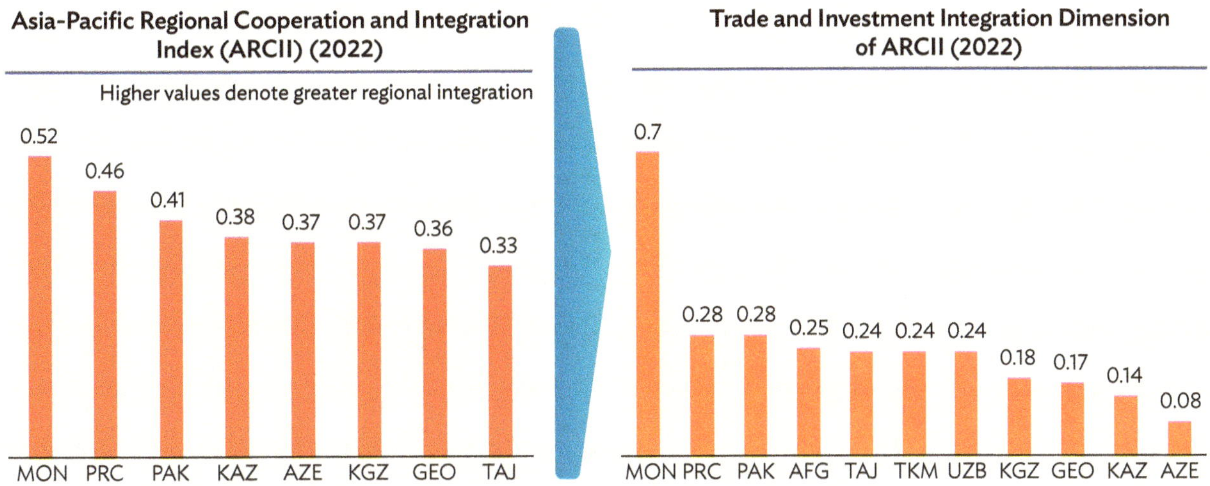

AFG = Afghanistan, AZE = Azerbaijan, PRC = The People's Republic of China, GEO = Georgia, KAZ = Kazakhstan, KGZ = Kyrgyz Republic, MON = Mongolia, PAK = Pakistan, TAJ = Tajikistan, TKM = Turkmenistan, UZB = Uzbekistan.

Note: Afghanistan, Turkmenistan, and Uzbekistan not mapped on ARCII 2022 Index.

Source: ADB–Asia Regional Integration Center Database. https://aric.adb.org/datacenter (accessed 25 April 2025).

The *trade and investment integration* dimension consists of five indicators: (i) proportion of intraregional goods exports to total goods exports, (ii) proportion of intraregional goods imports to total goods imports, (iii) intraregional trade intensity index, (iv) proportion of intraregional FDI inflows to total FDI inflows, and (v) proportion of intraregional FDI to total FDI. Mongolia ranks highest across all indicators except for two: the share of intraregional goods imports, where Afghanistan leads with a

[9] ARCII is a comprehensive metric developed to evaluate the progress and extent of regional cooperation and integration among countries in Asia and the Pacific region. This index is designed to assess how well countries are integrating economically, socially, and institutionally within the region. The index consists of 8 dimensions: trade and investment integration, money and finance integration, regional value chain, infrastructure and connectivity, people and social integration, institutional arrangements, technology and digital connectivity, and environmental cooperation.

score of 65.32, and the intraregional trade intensity index, where Turkmenistan ranks highest with a score of 2.12. Figure 5 depicts the top performing CAREC countries under the five indicators of the *trade and investment integration* dimension.

Figure 5: Top CAREC Countries on the Trade and Investment Integration Dimension

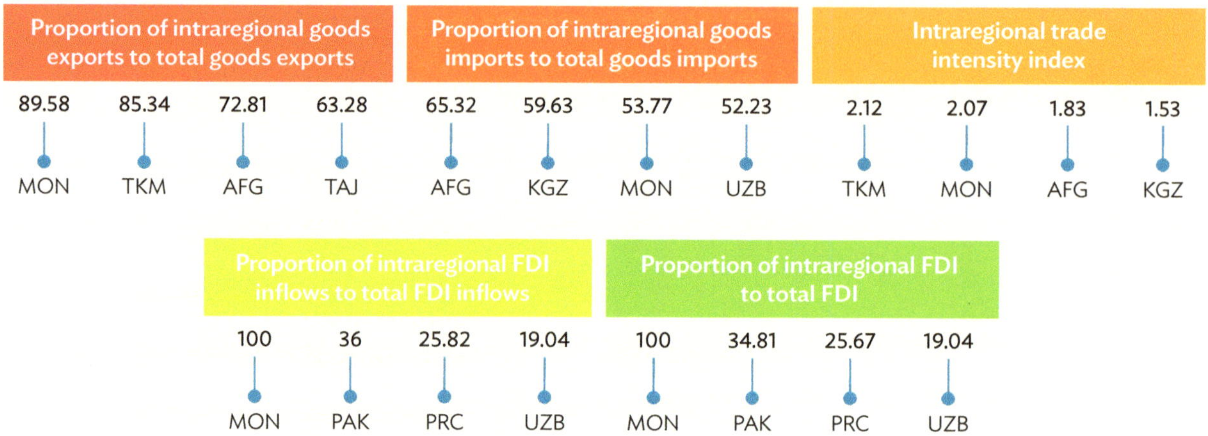

AFG = Afghanistan, CAREC = Central Asia Regional Economic Cooperation, PRC = People's Republic of China, FDI = foreign direct investment, KGZ = Kyrgyz Republic, MON =Mongolia, PAK =Pakistan, TAJ = Tajikistan, TKM = Turkmenistan, UZB = Uzbekistan.
Source: ADB–Asia Regional Integration Center Database. https://aric.adb.org/datacenter (accessed 25 April 2025).

Trade and transport facilitation is a priority area under CAREC 2030

Trade and transport connectivity, critical to regional integration, are key operational priorities for the CAREC 2030 framework as well. Accordingly, CAREC member countries adopted CAREC Integrated Trade Agenda 2030 (CITA), a trade strategy that takes a more synergistic approach to trade issues, focusing on providing greater market access, economic diversification, and strengthening the institutions for trade. Figure 6 highlights the three strategic pillars of CITA 2030.

CAREC countries have been working on modernizing customs procedures to simplify and standardize processes.It is adopting single window systems to streamline trade documentation and reduce delays at borders and it is developing and pilot testing the CAREC Customs Information Common Exchange and the CAREC Advanced Transit System. Implementation of the CAREC Common Agenda for Modernization of Sanitary and Phytosanitary (SPS) Measures for trade facilitation is underway to reduce nontariff barriers and facilitate smoother trade flows. Several CAREC countries have entered into bilateral and multilateral trade agreements to promote regional trade. These agreements aim to lower tariffs, reduce trade barriers, and promote economic cooperation.

Overall, regional cooperation in trade and transport facilitation among CAREC member countries is progressing, with significant achievements enhancing economic integration and connectivity.

Figure 6: CAREC Integrated Trade Agenda 2030 Strategic Pillars

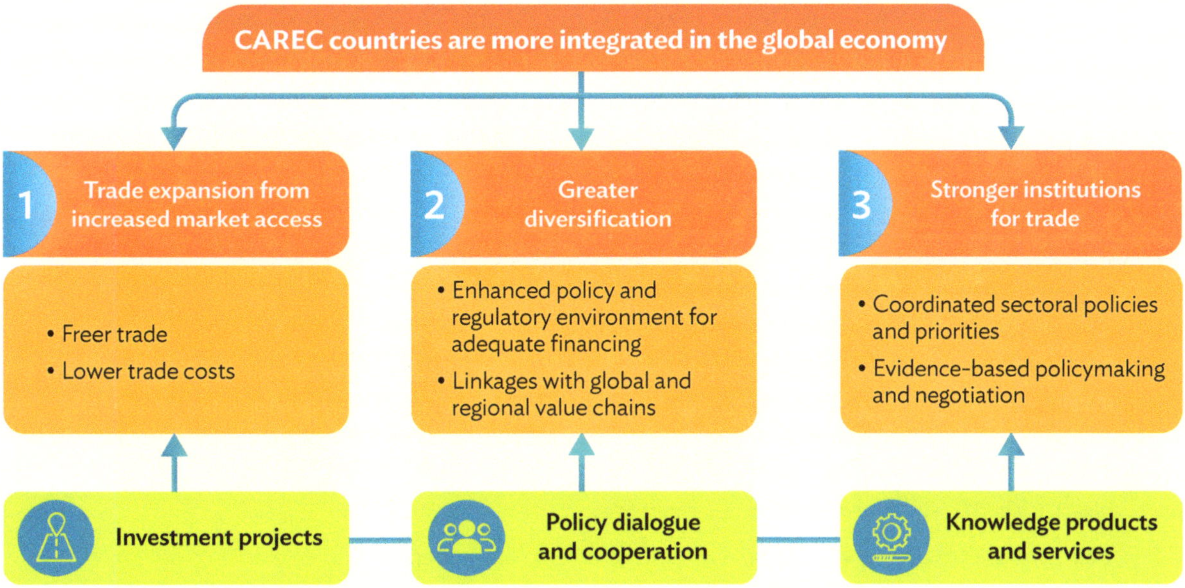

CAREC = Central Asia Regional Economic Cooperation.
Source: CAREC Integrated Trade Agenda (CITA) 2030

Overview of Corridor Performance Measurement and Monitoring and Its Role in Trade Facilitation in CAREC Region

The Corridor Performance Measurement and Monitoring (CPMM) mechanism is a critical tool for enhancing trade facilitation and transport efficiency in the CAREC region. It is an empirical tool designed by the CAREC Program in 2009 to assess and track the time and cost of moving goods across borders and along the six priority transport corridors spanning the 11 participating countries in the region. It focuses on identifying bottlenecks, inefficiencies, and barriers to trade and transport. Figure 7 clearly demonstrates the objectives of CPMM framework.

Figure 7: Objectives of Corridor Performance Measurement and Monitoring

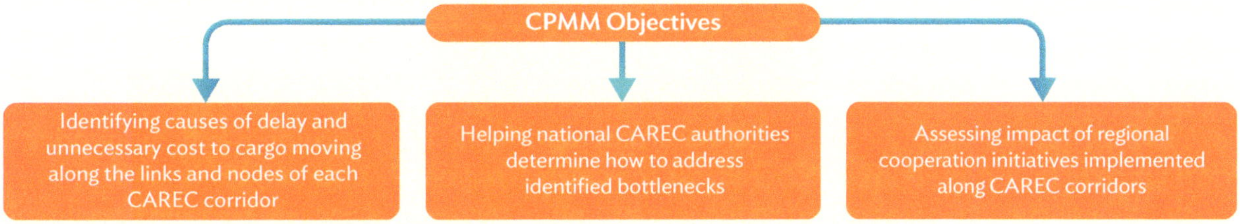

CAREC = Central Asia Regional Economic Cooperation, CPMM = corridor performance measurement and monitoring.
Source: ADB–CPMM methodology based on ESCAP time/cost/distance evaluation.

The CPMM methodology is based on a time and cost–distance framework, which lays out the cost and time components of door-to-door movements of a vehicle along a transport corridor and tracks delays at borders and other inspection points along the corridor. Its main trade facilitation indicators include (i) time to cross a border, (ii) cost to cross a border, (iii) total transport cost, and (iv) speeds. The analysis is decomposed into road and rail transport, and "at the border" and "behind border" (ADB 2022a, 2). Box 1 indicates the significance of each trade facilitation indicator.

Box 1: Trade Facilitation Indicators of Corridor Performance Measurement and Monitoring

1. **TFI 1 - Time taken to clear a border crossing point (BCP):** Average length of time (hours) it takes to move cargo across a border from entry to exit of a BCP. The intent is to capture the complexity and the inefficiencies inherent in the border-crossing process. This trade facilitation indicator (TFI) highlights bottlenecks at BCPs, which typically involve lengthy border-crossing procedures and serious delays.

2. **TFI 2 - Cost incurred at a BCP:** Average total cost of moving cargo across a border from entry to exit of a BCP, including both official and unofficial payments for 20 tons of cargo. This TFI highlights BCPs that have relatively expensive border-crossing procedures, including unofficial payments.

3. **TFI 3 - Cost incurred to travel a corridor section:** Average total costs, incurred for a unit (20 tons) of cargo traveling along a corridor section (500 kilometers) within a country or across borders including both official and unofficial payments. This TFI provides insight into the cost structure of a corridor and how that compares with other corridors.

4. **TFI 4 - Speed to travel along CAREC corridors:** Average speed at which a unit (20 tons) of cargo travels along a corridor section (500 kilometers) within a country or across borders based on total time spent on the journey. This TFI provides insight into the level of infrastructure present on the corridor by providing information on the total time taken for the entire journey including stoppage time for various reasons.

5. **Speed without delay:** Average speed at which a unit (20 tons) of cargo travels along a corridor section (500 kilometers) based on actual traveling time. This indicator provides insight into the level of transport infrastructure development of CAREC corridors by providing information on the speeds that cargo trucks and trains can attain while traversing specific corridor sections.

CAREC = Central Asia Regional Economic Cooperation, CPMM = corridor performance measurement and monitoring.
Source: ADB 2022a.

Significance of CPMM in trade facilitation and policymaking

The CPMM mechanism provides a standardized framework for measuring and monitoring the performance of transportation corridors across the CAREC region. By assessing corridor performance consistently, policymakers are able to identify opportunities for regional cooperation and development.

Further, like any performance measurement and monitoring system, the CPMM mechanism provides policymakers accurate and up-to-date information on corridor performance metrics, enabling them to make informed decisions, including where to allocate resources for infrastructure projects.

It is also a tool for evaluating policy and intervention effectiveness. By comparing performance metrics before and after policy implementation, policymakers can assess whether their strategies are achieving desired outcomes and adjust as necessary. Figure 8 explains CPMM methodology for evaluating project impact analysis across countries.

Figure 8: Use of Corridor Performance Measurement and Monitoring in Evaluating Project Impact Across CAREC Countries

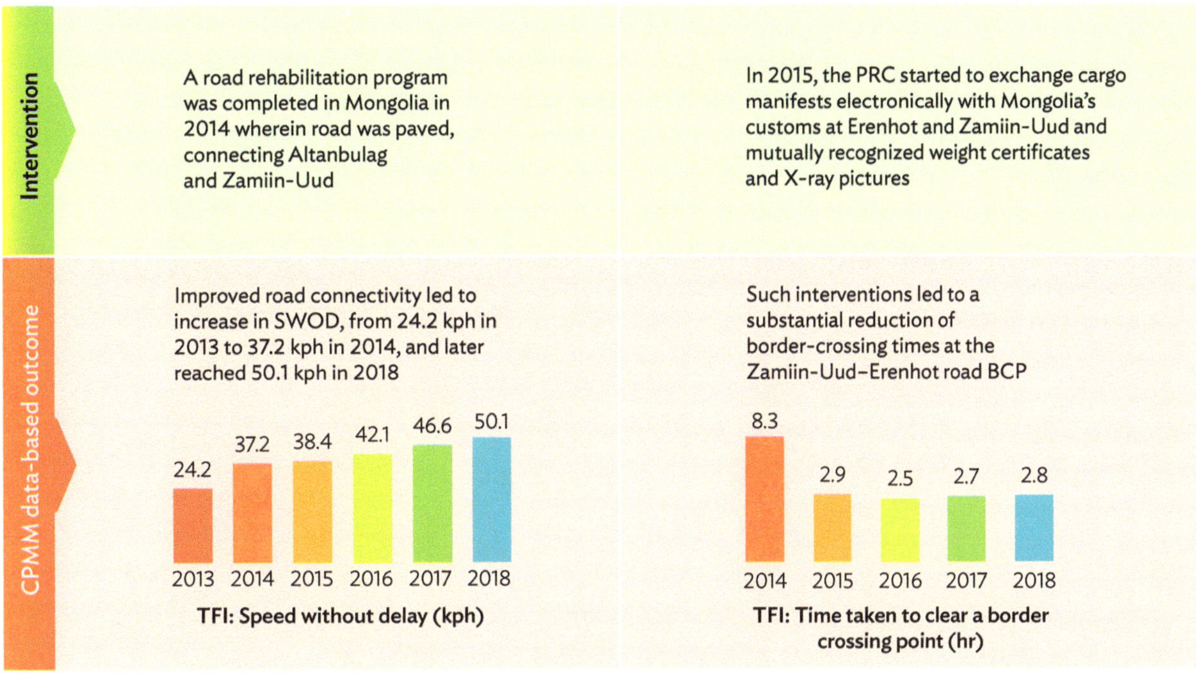

ADB = Asian Development Bank, BCP = border crossing point, CAREC = Central Asia Regional Economic Cooperation, PRC = People's Republic of China, CPMM = corridor performance measurement and monitoring, hr = hour, kph = kilometer per hour, SWOD = speed without delay, TFI = trade facilitation indicator.

Source: Study team's analysis based on ADB 2022a.

Overall, the CAREC CPMM provides crucial insights in policymaking that can enhance regional cooperation, trade facilitation, and infrastructure development. While the CPMM effectively captures outcome-level indicators—such as time, cost, and speed of movement—it is not designed to diagnose the underlying causes of inefficiencies. To build on its strengths, this study examines the CPMM framework in relation to broader trade and transport facilitation themes (outlined in section 3) to generate more granular insights into specific bottlenecks at the BCP level. This complementary approach seeks to enrich the existing evidence base and support more targeted policy interventions.

2 Objectives of the Study

Objectives of the Study

The study aims mainly to expand the existing CPMM framework for evaluating the extent of trade and transport facilitation at border crossing points (BCPs). It aim not only to improve the effectiveness of the Asian Development Bank (ADB) project implementation but also to support broader government policymaking efforts across members. To achieve this, the study focused on several key thematic areas critical to trade and transport facilitation at BCPs:

(i) **Customs procedures and formalities:** This addresses the simplification and standardization of customs processes to reduce delays and increase transparency. It includes assessment of procedures involved in documentation, risk management systems, and clearance methods to enhance the speed and security of cargo processing at borders.

(ii) **Customs coordination:** This focuses on harmonizing customs practices across borders to foster seamless trade by enhancing communication and synchronizing operations between neighboring countries' customs administrations. It includes evaluating the level of coordination and identifying procedural redundancies, while highlighting practices that facilitate smoother cross-border trade, such as mutual agreements and integrated digital systems.

(iii) **Transit cross-border support facilities:** This highlights the availability and advancement of key infrastructure required for efficient cross-border movement of goods, including land customs stations, dry ports, bonded warehouses, and quarantine and/or testing facilities. These support facilities play a critical role in securely storing, inspecting, and managing goods in transit, thereby minimizing bottlenecks and enhancing the overall flow of trade.

(iv) **Transport regulations**: This focuses on aligning transport policies and regulations to support the movement of vehicles and cargo across borders. Key areas of assessment include licensing, vehicle standards, driver regulations, and harmonizing transport laws to minimize regulatory discrepancies.

Based on these thematic areas, the study aimed to develop a comprehensive framework for evaluating trade and transport facilitation at BCPs in CAREC countries. A more structured and in-depth evaluation framework would help provide better insights into operational challenges and opportunities at the borders, helping assess the impact of ADB projects while also guiding national governments in policymaking.

Through this comprehensive evaluation framework, the study seeks to contribute to more effective trade and transport facilitation, improved cross-border operations, and overall economic growth in the CAREC region.

Framework of Analysis

The study employs a structured, six-workstream approach to evaluate trade and transport facilitation (Figure 9).

Figure 9: Approach of the Study

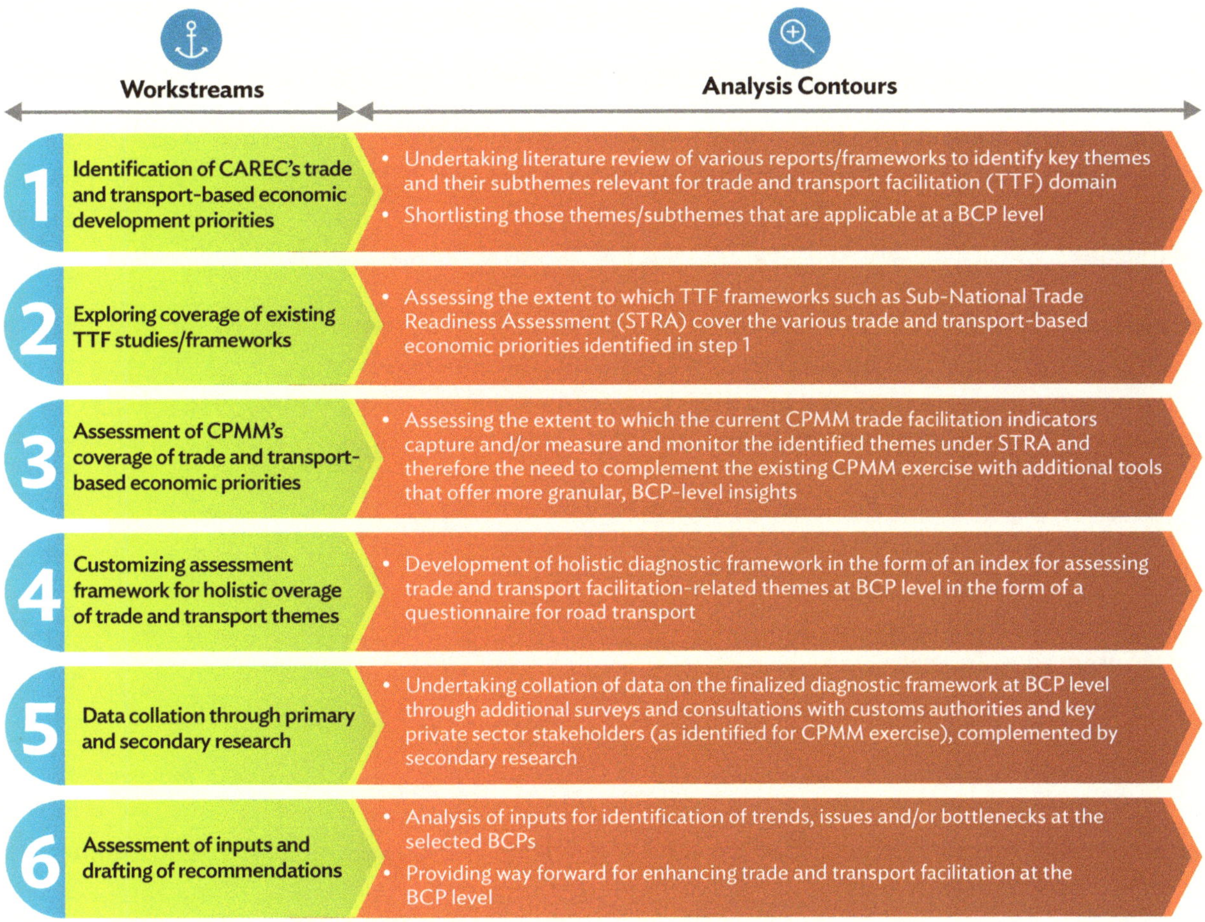

BCP = border crossing point, CAREC = Central Asia Regional Economic Cooperation, CPMM = corridor performance measurement and monitoring.

Source: Study team's approach to the study.

Workstream 1 entailed understanding CAREC's trade-based economic development priorities through a literature review of CAREC vision documents and other trade and transport facilitation (TTF)-related publications for the CAREC region. This included identification of various TTF themes and subthemes relevant for the region, and shortlisting those that could be measured at BCP level in CAREC countries.

Workstream 2 assessed the extent to which ADB's Sub-national Trade Readiness Assessment framework—as designed in the *Integrated Approach to Trade and Transport Facilitation: Measuring Readiness for Sustainable, Inclusive, and Resilient Trade*—covers the various trade and transport-based economic priorities identified in workstream 1 to understand its relevance in the present context.

Having established the comprehensive nature of the Sub-national Trade Readiness Assessment in covering TTF priority themes for the CAREC region, **Workstream 3** involved mapping CPMM trade facilitation indicators to Sub-national Trade Readiness Assessment's TTF themes. This process aimed to assess the need to complement the existing CPMM exercise with additional tools that offer more granular, BCP-level insights to evaluate the trade facilitation scenario.

Based on the analysis in Workstream 3, **Workstream 4** developed a comprehensive Cross-Border Trade and Transport Facilitation Index to evaluate the preparedness of BCPs to facilitate trade and transport effectively. This index was modeled along the lines of Sub-national Trade Readiness Assessment for road transport BCPs, and a survey questionnaire was formulated for collating the requisite data.

Workstream 5 conducted fieldwork through surveys (from September 2024 to January 2025) and consultations with customs authorities and key private sector stakeholders (as identified for CPMM exercise), to collect data in survey questionnaire complemented by secondary research to complete the picture of the subnational trade environment.

For this study, the following BCPs were assessed:

(i) Kirmizi Korpu, Azerbaijan
(ii) Tsiteli Khidi, Georgia
(iii) Serhetabat, Turkmenistan
(iv) Farap, Turkmenistan
(v) Torkham, Pakistan
(vi) Yallama, Uzbekistan

These crossings were selected based on data availability and quality, ensuring assessments could be performed for at least one pair of BCPs (Kirmizi Korpu, Azerbaijan, and Tsiteli Khidi, Georgia), apart from facilitating intra-country comparisons (Serhetabat and Farap, Turkmenistan) as well as inter-country comparisons (Torkham, Pakistan; Yallama, Uzbekistan; and the others mentioned).

Workstream 6 focused on analyzing the Cross-Border Trade and Transport Facilitation Index based on the primary survey and secondary inputs for identifying the bottlenecks and opportunities for improvement for the selected BCP themes such as customs procedures and formalities, customs coordination, transit and cross-border support facilities, and transport regulations.

This comprehensive evaluation framework helps offer actionable insights for policymakers and stakeholders to enhance the efficiency and effectiveness of cross border trade, ultimately contributing to smoother and more efficient trade flows at the regional level.

3 Literature Review

Review of Existing Studies to Identify Trade and Transport Facilitation Themes

The review of the existing literature on CAREC trade and transport facilitation included CAREC Integrated Trade Agenda 2030 (CITA 2030), Rolling Strategic Action Plans, focus areas for Customs Cooperation Committee, CITA 2030 Results Framework as well as the National Trade Readiness Assessment parameters (ADB's Integrated Approach to Trade and Transport Facilitation, 2022) which could be applied at the subnational (border crossing point) level.

CAREC Integrated Trade Agenda 2030

CITA 2030 is a strategic initiative aimed at enhancing trade and economic integration among the CAREC member countries. This agenda focuses on three key pillars: trade expansion, trade diversification, and trade facilitation (Box 2) with emphasis on digital trade and adoption of new technologies to streamline customs procedures and enhance cross-border e-commerce. By reducing trade barriers, improving infrastructure, and promoting regulatory reforms, CITA 2030 seeks to increase the competitiveness of member countries in the global market.

As part of this study, the key focus areas under each of the strategic pillars were mapped to identify and understand the priority areas for trade and transport facilitation in the CAREC region. Figure 10 presents the resulting TTF themes, which are anchored in these strategic pillars.

Box 2: Pillars Under CITA 2030

Pillar 1: Trade expansion from increased market access
The CAREC Integrated Trade Agenda (CITA) aims to enhance market access through adopting open trade policies with customs cooperation and integrated trade facilitation. The pillar includes measures to lower tariffs, eliminate nontariff barriers which promotes free trade. Additionally, the pillar includes measures to make border and behind-the-border procedures more efficient, improve logistics services, and enhance transit systems to lower trade costs. It emphasizes customs simplification and harmonization, paperless trade initiatives, implementation of transit schemes such as the CAREC advanced transit system, integrated border management, etc.

continued on next page

Box 2 *continued*

Pillar 2: Greater diversification

CITA has goals for enabling greater economic diversification environment through enhanced policy and regulatory measures with adequate financing. There are initiatives to establish a multilateral agency for trade finance that helps to improve small and medium-sized enterprises access to trade finance including the Asian Development Bank's Trade and Supply Chain Finance Program and trade insurance.

Pillar 3: Stronger institutions for trade

The pillar focuses on promoting coordination of sectoral policies and priorities backed by evidence-based policymaking. There are planned measures for collaborative policy formulation and implementation, alignment of national with regional planning, and regulatory convergence among members. CITA will improve data management and cross-country analysis, enhance the policy analysis and negotiation skills of officials, and increase think tank and private sector participation.

Source: CAREC Integrated Trade Agenda 2030. https://www.carecprogram.org/uploads/CAREC-Integrated-Trade-Agenda-2030.pdf.

Figure 10: Trade and Transport Facilitation Themes Covered Under CITA 2030

Pillar	Focus Areas	Trade and Transport Facilitation Theme
Trade expansion from increased market access	Lower tariffs, elimination of nontariff barriers to trade, making at-the-border and behind-the-border procedures more efficient, improving logistics services, enhancing transit systems, and limiting trade-distorting and protectionist measures.	Customs procedures efficiency and cross-border harmonization Customs automation Transit systems, infrastructure and SPS facilities
Greater diversification	Improvement of access to trade finance, instituting consistent and open FDI policies, developing domestic financial markets, strengthening support services, upgrading skills, and nurturing innovation.	Access to trade finance
Stronger institutions for trade	Improving data management and cross-country analysis, enhancing policy analysis and negotiation skills of officials, and increasing think tank and private sector participation	Institutional and human resources development
Sustainable trade (cross-cutting theme)		

FDI = foreign direct investment, SPS = sanitary and phytosanitary.

Source: Study team's analysis based on the CAREC Integrated Trade Agenda (CITA) 2030.

The CITA 2030 Results Framework, which provides a structured approach to monitoring and evaluating the progress and impact of the CITA 2030 was also reviewed. It outlines specific goals, targets, and indicators across three key pillars: trade expansion, trade facilitation, and trade diversification.

Rolling Strategic Action Plans

The CAREC Rolling Strategic Action Plan was designed to implement the priorities of the CITA 2030 strategy trade and transport infrastructure. This plan aimed to enhance regional cooperation by addressing critical challenges such as infrastructure gaps, regulatory barriers, and economic diversification. Key initiatives included improving transport corridors, streamlining customs procedures, and fostering strengthened institutions in the region.

The strategic projects under the Rolling Strategic Action Plan were mapped to key TTF themes to identify focus areas for the CAREC region as shown in Figure 11.

Figure 11: Transport and Trade Facilitation Under the Rolling Strategic Action Plan

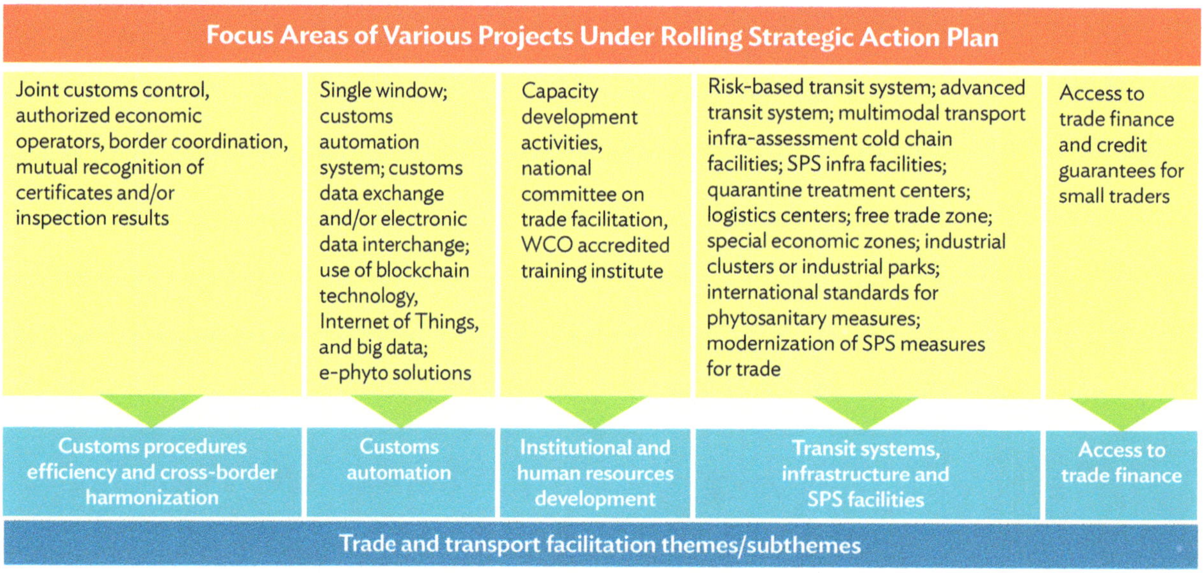

SPS = sanitary and phytosanitary, TTF = transport and trade facilitation, WCO = World Customs Organization.
Source: Study team's analysis based on CAREC RSAP.

Focus Areas of the Customs Cooperation Committee

The CAREC Customs Cooperation Committee focuses on enhancing regional customs cooperation to facilitate trade and secure supply chains across member countries. Key areas of attention include harmonizing customs procedures, adopting international standards, and implementing advanced technologies such as electronic data interchange systems. The Customs Cooperation Committee works to streamline border processes, reduce clearance times, and combat illicit trade by improving risk management and enforcement capabilities. Additionally, the committee promotes capacity building and knowledge sharing among customs authorities to foster a more efficient, transparent, and interconnected customs environment in the CAREC region. The strategic focus areas of the Customs Cooperation Committee mapped to the key TTF thematic areas are given in Figure 12.

Figure 12: Trade and Transport Facilitation Themes Based on Focus Areas of Customs Cooperation Committee

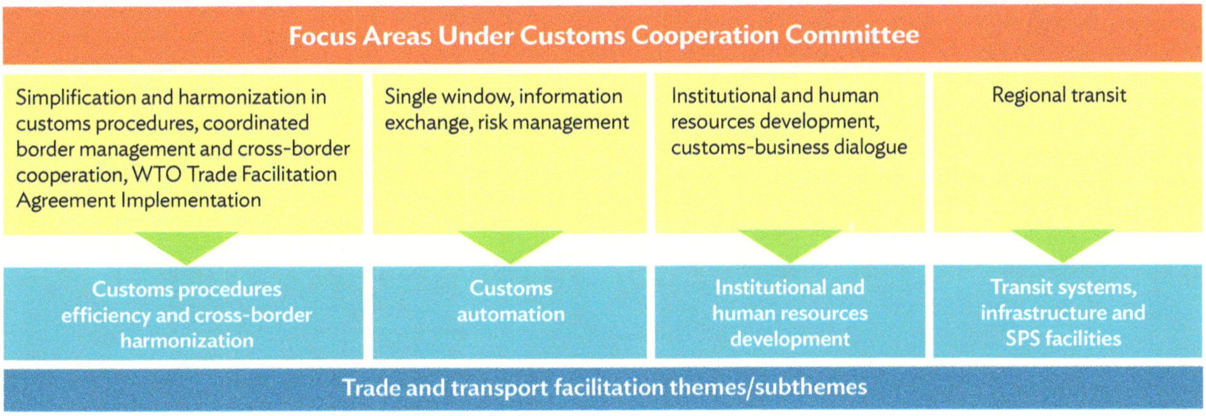

SPS = sanitary and phytosanitary, WTO = World Trade Organization.
Source: Study team's analysis based on the CAREC Customs Cooperation Committee.

Themes Under National Trade Readiness Assessment Applicable at the Border Crossing Point Level

The National Trade Readiness Assessment is a diagnostic tool designed in the report: "Integrated Approach to Trade and Transport Facilitation" to evaluate a country's preparedness to engage in and benefit from international trade. It examines various factors, including trade policies, regulatory frameworks, infrastructure, and institutional capacities, to identify strengths and areas needing improvement. The assessment provides a comprehensive analysis of the trade environment, highlighting key challenges such as tariff and nontariff barriers, logistical inefficiencies, and gaps in trade facilitation measures. The list of parameters applicable at the BCP level as well have been mapped to key TTF thematic areas, as shown in Figure 13.

Figure 13: Key Themes Under National Trade Readiness Assessment at the Border Crossing Point Level

Focus Areas of Various Projects Under RSAP				
Cross-border harmonization, adherence to international standards for customs, authorized operators program, procedures simplification, mutual recognition agreements	Single window implementation, electronic declaration systems, digital certificates, automated risk management, electronic payment	Institutionalized mechanism to support interagency coordination, coordinated infrastructure use, cross border staff training programs	Established procedures for pre-arrival processing, automated processing of customs declaration, quality of trade and transport infrastructure	Accessibility of customs financing provisions
Customs procedures efficiency and cross-border harmonization	Customs automation	Institutional and human resources development	Transit systems, infrastructure and SPS facilities	Access to trade finance
Trade and transport facilitation themes/subthemes				

RSAP = Rolling Strategic Action Plan, SPS = sanitary and phytosanitary.
Source: Study team's analysis based on ADB 2022b.

Based on the review and analysis of these reports/publications, the various TTF related focus areas identified as priorities for the CAREC region were mapped to the six broad TTF thematic areas presented in Figure 14.

Figure 14: Mapping Themes Covered Under CAREC Frameworks/Reports

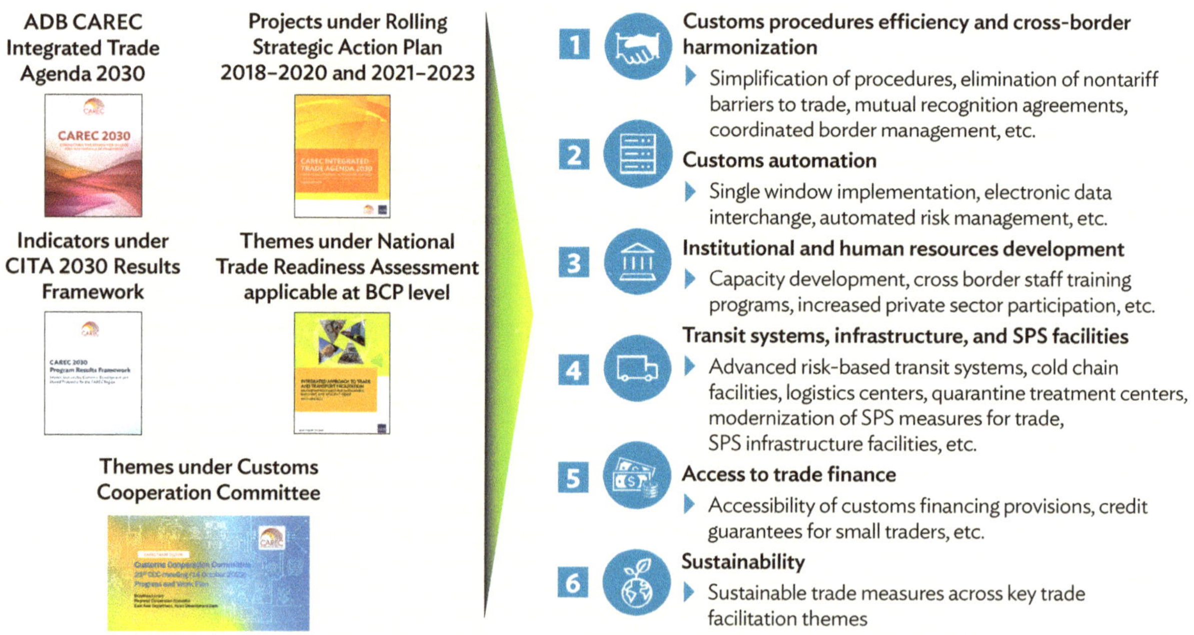

ADB = Asian Development Bank, BCP = border crossing point, CAREC = Central Asia Regional Economic Cooperation, CITA = CAREC Integrated Trade Agenda, SPS = sanitary and phytosanitary.
Source: Study team's analysis.

The themes identified as key CAREC priorities in TTF were compared with the themes of Sub-national Trade Readiness Assessment as per the Integrated Approach to Trade and Transport Facilitation. It was found that the trade and transport facilitation themes identified under ADB (2022b) align with CAREC's priority areas identified above. This comparison is clearly illustrated in Figure 15.

Figure 15: Comparing Themes Identified in CAREC Region and Those in Transport and Trade Facilitation Study

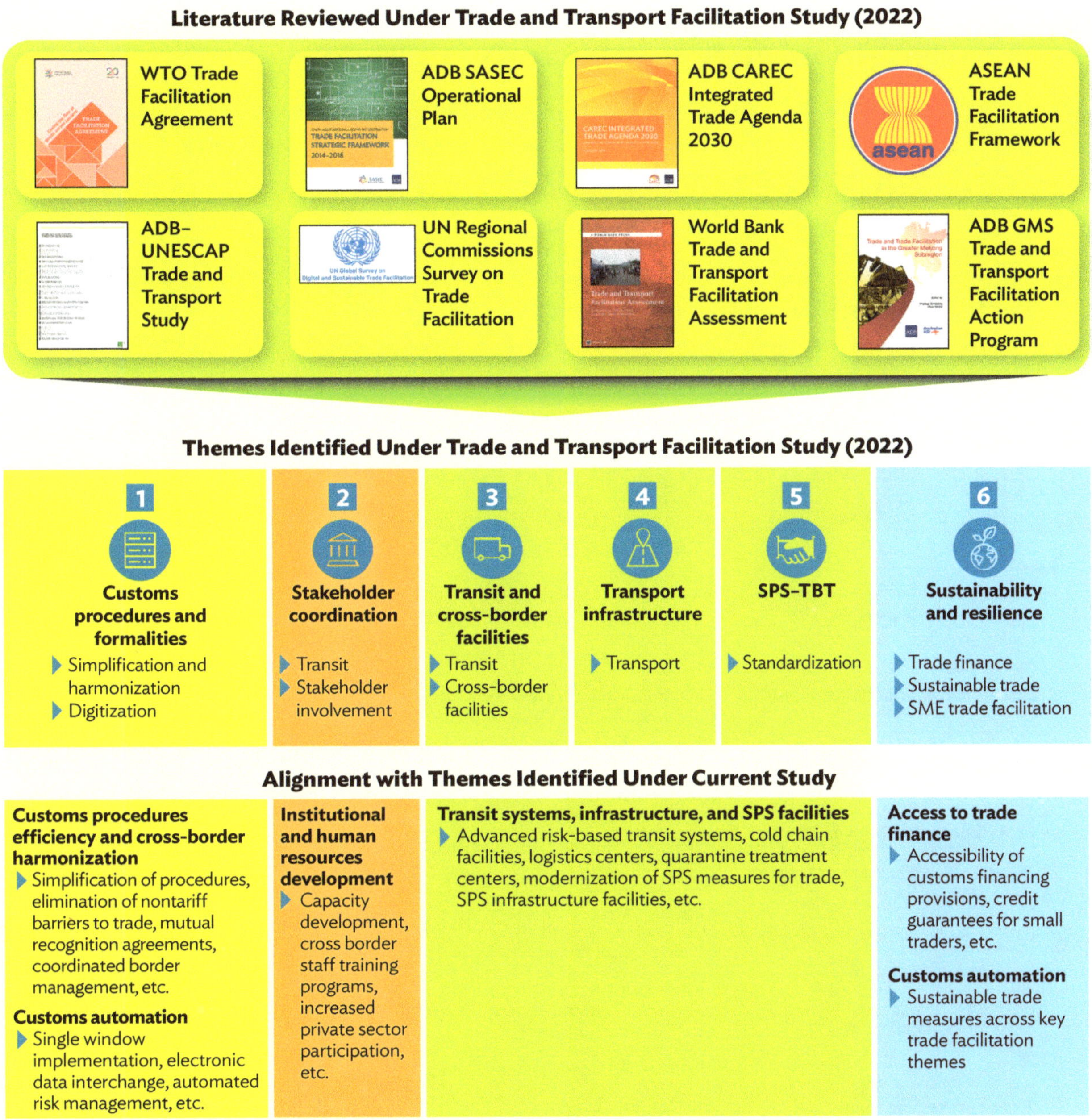

ADB = Asian Development Bank, ASEAN = Association of Southeast Asian Nations, CAREC = Central Asia Regional Economic Cooperation, GMS = Greater Mekong Subregion, SASEC = South Asia Subregional Economic Cooperation, SME = small and medium-sized enterprise, SPS = sanitary and phytosanitary, TBT = technical barriers to trade, UN = United Nations, UNESCAP = United Nations Economic and Social Commission for Asia and the Pacific, WTO = World Trade Organization.

Source: Study team's analysis.

The theme mapping given in Figure 15 suggests the relevance of Sub-national Trade Readiness Assessment for the trade and transport evaluation at CAREC region BCPs.

Identification of Research Gaps

The CAREC region evaluates CAREC trade corridor performance through the CPMM framework. While the Sub-national Trade Readiness Assessment covers 43 parameters across the six thematic areas to evaluate the trade and transport facilitation scenario, an analysis of the CPMM's coverage of parameters of the framework revealed that only 13 of 43 parameters in the framework are covered by the CPMM (either directly/indirectly/partially) (Table 1).

Table 1: Analysis of Corridor Performance Measurement and Monitoring Coverage of Subnational Trade Readiness Assessment

S. No.	Themes	Query	Coverage under CPMM
Customs Procedures and Formalities and Stakeholder Coordination			
1	**Customs clearance process**	What is the average time taken for import clearance?	Y
2		What percentage of import declarations are cleared electronically?	N
3		What is the average time taken for export clearance?	Y
4		What percentage of export declarations are cleared electronically?	N
5		Is duplication of bureaucratic activities prevalent?	N
6		What is the cost of border clearance?	Y
7		Is there provision of digital payment of duties and taxes?	N
8	**Pre-shipment inspection**	What is the total time taken for pre-shipment physical inspection?	Y
9		What is the percentage of physical inspection?	N
10	**Solicitation of informal payments**	Is informal payments prevalent at cargo clearance/checkpoints/ weighbridge stations/traffic stops, etc.?	Y
11	**Cross border coordination**	Are the border timings, clearance procedures synchronized?	N
12		Are the borders crossings governed by international agreements?	N
Transit Cross-Border Facilities and SPS-TBT			
13	**Warehousing/transloading facilities**	What is the total no. of warehousing facilities in the vicinity?	N
14		Is transshipment yard present?	Y
15		What is the cost of warehousing and transloading	Partial
16		Is warehousing/transloading process compulsory?	N
17	**Telecommunications and IT**	Is ICT Infrastructure present?	N
18		Is Internet and mobile connectivity available at the location?	N
19	**Export processing zones**	What is the total number of SEZs/manufacturing facilities in the vicinity?	N
20		Are custom bonded warehouses available in the vicinity?	N

continued on next page

Table 1 *continued*

S. No.	Themes	Query	Coverage under CPMM
21	**Quality/standards inspection agencies**	Is inspection facility available?	Partial
22		Is IT-based risk management system operational?	N
23	**Health/SPS agencies**	Is quarantine facility available?	Partial
24	**Other facilities**	Are facilities such as X-rays, scanners, weighbridges, etc. available at the crossing point?	N
Transport Infrastructure and Sustainability and Resilience			
25	**Maritime transport**	What are the fees charged by port?	N
26		What is the annual capacity of the port?	N
27		What is the total no. of available terminals?	N
28		What is the total no. of available berths?	N
29		What is the utilization percentage of the port?	N
30		What is the size of containers handled?	N
31	**Road**	Is the BCP connected to a national highway/carriageway/expressway?	N
32		What is the type of laning of the connecting road?	N
33		Is a parking area available in the vicinity?	N
34		What is the total volume of cargo trucks exchanged per day?	N
35		What is the rate of road transport? (transport charges, in USD)	Partial
36		What is the average time taken for cross border cargo transport?	Y
37	**Rail**	Is operational rail line and haul infrastructure present at the BCP?	Y
38		What are the rail transport rates?	Partial
39		What is the type of rail gauge in use?	N
40	**Air transport**	What are the charges for cargo transit by airport?	N
41		What is the time taken for cargo processing?	N
42	**Freight forwarders/logistics service providers/shippers**	What are the freight forwarding charges? (per TEU)	N
43		What are the types of trucks/cargo vehicles used? (use of environment friendly vehicles)	N

BCP = border crossing point, CPMM = corridor performance measurement and monitoring, ICT = information and communication technology, IT = information technology, N = No, SEZ = special economic zone, SPS = sanitary and phytosanitary, SPS–TBT = sanitary and phytosanitary–technical barriers to trade, STRA = sub-national trade readiness assessment, TEU = twenty-foot equivalent unit, USD = United States dollars, Y = Yes.

Source: Study team's analysis based on ADB 2022b.

The above analysis indicates the potential for complementing the CPMM framework to evaluate the trade facilitation scenario at the BCP level. Based on this analysis, potential suggestions to expand the CPMM framework are recommended in the next chapter.

4 Trade Facilitation Readiness Assessment at Subnational Level

Structure of Assessment Framework

The CPMM consists of four trade facilitation indicators measuring time, cost, and speed elements at BCP and corridor level. As per the previous section, the data from these trade facilitation indicators cover 13 of 43 parameters of the Sub-National Trade Readiness Assessment. To complement the CPMM framework in view of the CAREC 2030 TTF priorities, a Cross-Border Trade and Transport Facilitation Index (CBTTFI) has been proposed as a composite Index under CPMM for evaluating various trade and transport facilitation related themes.

The CBTTFI is based on Sub-National Trade Readiness Assessment framework adopted from previous ADB–TTF study and customized to suit the needs and requirements of the CAREC region. The objective of this index is to help supplement the current trade facilitation indicators with more granular information at the BCP level, helping trade analysts and policymakers understand the reasons behind high trade time and costs at the border points. Additionally, the index will help facilitate comparisons of both intra-country and inter-country border points within the CAREC region using standardized parameters.

Key pillars on which the CBTTFI is based:

(i) **At the border and behind the border infrastructure:** The evaluation is based on the availability of the "at the border" infrastructure including:

- (a) parking,
- (b) warehousing and/or logistics,
- (c) testing and/or certification, and
- (d) material handling, etc. The evaluation also includes aspects about "behind the border" including transport infrastructure, logistics connectivity among others.

(v) **Institutions:** The parameter aims to evaluate the level of efficiency and coordination among various stakeholders and/or institutions, including partner government agencies, customs officials of neighboring BCPs, etc., to analyze the impact on competency and quality of services (cost and lead time) provided by each of the institutions in cross border transit.

(vi) **Policies and regulations:** The evaluation would be based on the level of implementation and impact of policies and regulations on the cross-border trade and transit activities such as submission of documents at customs, processing of export–import clearances, digitalization levels across activities among other activities.

Based on these pillars, the CBTTFI covers four key themes and 10 subthemes of trade and transport facilitation via road at a BCP (Figure 16).

Figure 16: Themes Under the Cross-Border Trade and Transport Facilitation Index

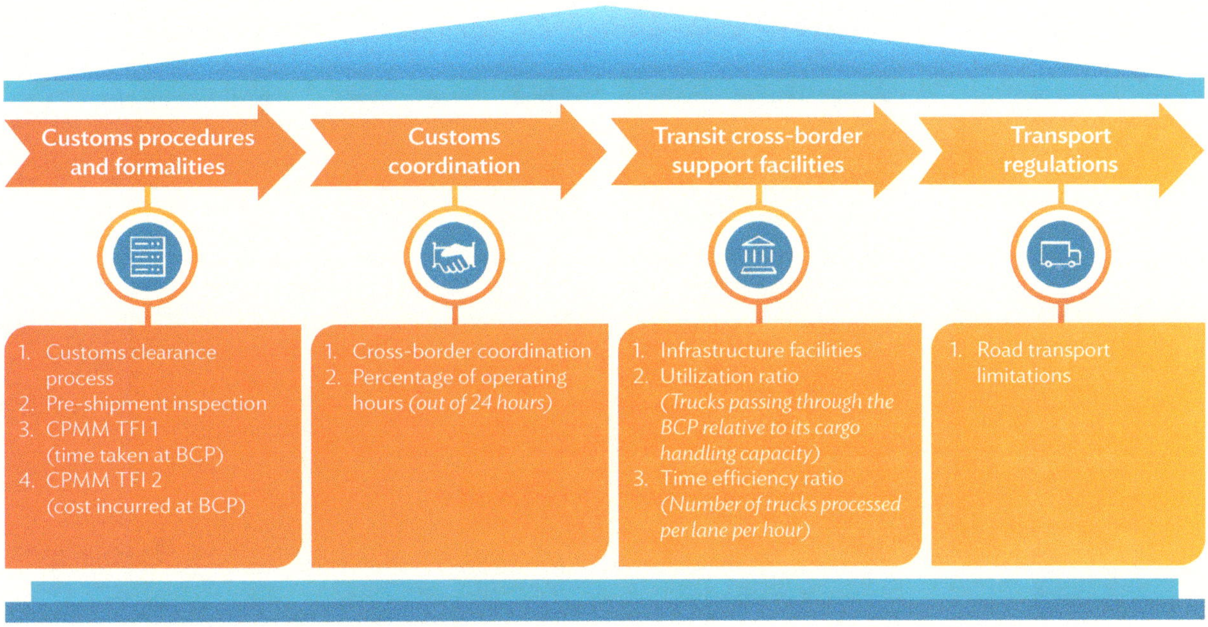

BCP = border crossing point, CPMM = corridor performance measurement and monitoring, TFI = trade facilitation indicator.
Source: Study team's proposal based on Sub-National Trade Readiness Assessment framework.

Building on these themes and subthemes, the CBTTFI enables policymakers to go beyond the CPMM data findings by uncovering the underlying reasons for high costs or delays across various activities identified in the CPMM analysis. This deeper insight facilitates the identification of key challenges and bottlenecks at specific BCPs.

Table 2 maps various activities for which cost and time elements are captured under CPMM to the elements recorded in the CBTTFI. This mapping helps identify the root causes of delays or high costs at BCPs.

Table 2: Mapping of Corridor Performance Measurement and Monitoring Activities with Cross-Border Trade and Transport Facilitation Index Components and Themes

S. No.	CPMM Activities	CBTTFI Components	CBTTFI Theme
1	Border security control	**Electronic processing of requisite documents:** Customs declaration, bill of lading, CMR consignment note, certificate of origin, packing list/cargo manifest, commercial invoice, TIR carnet/customs bond	●
		Presence of ICT infrastructure: Single window portal, automated customs management system, e-TIR, e-CMR, customs mobile app, electronic queue management, interoperable systems between customs authorities	●
2	Customs control	**Pre-arrival processing:** Documentation submission, risk assessment-based inspections, advance fee payment for inspections	●
		Automated risk assessment: System for computerized risk-based assessment for inspections; percentage of physical inspection	●
		Customs staff capacity: Availability of sufficient staff available for undertaking inspections at BCPs	●
		Customs valuation based on World Trade Organization: Customs valuation based on World Trade Organization Agreement on Customs Valuation; consistency of customs classification among customs headquarters and border branch offices	●
		Joint customs control operations and mutual recognition of documents: Interoperable information systems, synchronized clearance, electronic data interchange	●
3	Commercial inspection	**Electronic processing of requisite documents:** Commercial inspection certificate, SPS certificate	●
		Presence of ICT infrastructure: Automated systems for SPS inspection, nonintrusive cargo inspection equipment	●
4	Health/quarantine	**Pre-arrival processing:** Prior intimation of testing and/or certification requirements, pre-arrival clearance	●
		Automated risk assessment: System for computerized risk-based assessment for inspections; percentage of physical inspection	●
5	Phytosanitary	**Customs staff capacity:** Availability of sufficient staff available for undertaking inspections at BCPs	●
		Joint customs control operations and mutual recognition of documents: Mutual recognition of inspection certificates, SPS certificates	●
6	Veterinary inspection	**Industrial/logistical infrastructure at the BCP/in the vicinity:** Quarantine treatment centers, certification and testing infrastructure, product testing laboratories	●
7	Visa/immigration	**Electronic processing of requisite documents:** Passport/national ID card, Visa	●
		Presence of ICT infrastructure: Automated passport control systems	●
8	Transit conformity	**Electronic processing of requisite documents:** Certificate of liability insurance, certificate of cargo insurance, commercial driver's license	●
		Presence of ICT infrastructure: Video surveillance, radiation detection, portable illegal drug identification systems	●
9	GAI/traffic inspection	**Industrial/logistical infrastructure at the BCP/in the vicinity:** Stand-by electric power generators, material handling equipment for heavy cargo	●
10	Police checkpoint/stop	**Automated risk assessment:** System for computerized risk-based assessment for inspections; percentage of physical inspection	●

continued on next page

Table 2 *continued*

S. No.	CPMM Activities	CBTTFI Components	CBTTFI Theme
11	Transport inspection	**Customs staff capacity:** Availability of sufficient staff available for undertaking inspections at BCPs	● customs procedures and formalities
12	Escort/convoy	**Joint customs control operations and mutual recognition of documents:** Recognition of AEO certification, vehicle registration, driver's license, insurance documents	● customs coordination
13	Weight/standard inspection	**Electronic processing of requisite documents:** Official weight ticket, certificate of standard conformance	● customs procedures and formalities
		Weight limit for cargo vehicles	● transport regulations
		Automated risk assessment: System for computerized risk-based assessment for inspections; percentage of physical inspection	● customs procedures and formalities
		Customs staff capacity: Availability of sufficient staff available for undertaking inspections at BCPs	● customs procedures and formalities
		Industrial/logistical infrastructure at the BCP/in the vicinity: Weighbridges	● transit cross border support facilities
14	Vehicle registration	**Electronic processing of requisite documents:** Vehicle registration document, permit for vehicle entry	● customs procedures and formalities
		Joint customs control operations and mutual recognition of documents: Recognition of AEO certification, vehicle registration, driver's license, insurance documents	● customs coordination
15	Emergency repair	**Industrial/logistical infrastructure at the BCP/in the vicinity:** Maintenance-repair facilities for vehicles	● transit cross border support facilities
16	Loading and unloading	**Industrial/logistical infrastructure at the BCP/in the vicinity:** Cargo transloading terminals	● transit cross border support facilities
17	Road/bridge toll	**Presence of ICT infrastructure:** Electronic payment/digital payment of duties and taxes	● customs procedures and formalities
18	Waiting/queueing	**Presence of ICT infrastructure:** Electronic queue management systems	● customs procedures and formalities
		Utilization Ratio Number of lanes exclusively for truck examination Expected increase in traffic over next 5 years	● transit cross border support facilities

● = customs procedures and formalities, ● = customs coordination, ● = transit cross border support facilities, ● = transport regulations.

AEO = authorized economic operator, BCP = border crossing point, CBTTFI = Cross-Border Trade and Transport Facilitation Index, CPMM = corridor performance measurement and monitoring, GAI = Gosudarstvennaya Avtomobilnaya Inspektsiya (State Automobile Inspectorate in Russian), e-CMR = electronic consignment note, ICT = information and communication technology, ID card = identification card, SPS = sanitary and phytosanitary, TIR = Transports Internationaux Routiers (International Road Transport).

Source: Study team's mapping based on the Corridor Performance Measurement and Monitoring methodology.

Contours of Fieldwork for Data Collection

The CBTTFI collects data through primary survey-based responses to a structured questionnaire covering identified themes, supplemented by secondary research to provide a comprehensive view of the subnational trade environment.

The primary stakeholders for data collection are the customs authorities of CAREC region countries. However, input from the private sector, including trade and transport associations, is also incorporated to complement the information provided by customs authorities. Accordingly, two distinct survey questionnaires have been developed—one for public sector stakeholders and another for private sector stakeholders—to capture relevant inputs for the CBTTFI. The questionnaires are in the Annex.

For undertaking the assessment, six BCPs—Kirmizi Korpu (Azerbaijan), Tsiteli Khidi (Georgia), Serhetabat and Farap (Turkmenistan), Torkham (Pakistan), and Yallama (Uzbekistan) were shortlisted (Figure 17).

Figure 17: Border Crossing Points Selected for the Assessment

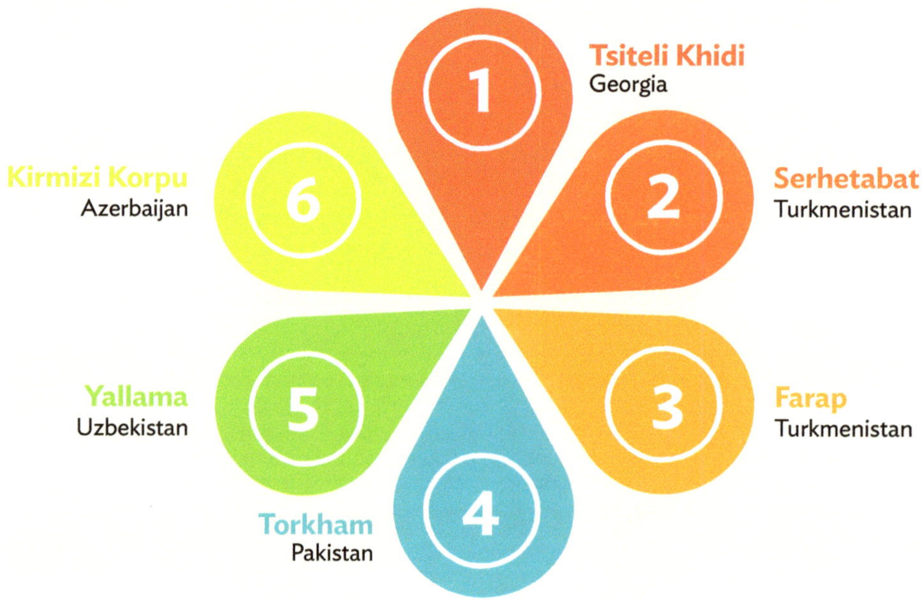

Source: Study team selection for the analysis.

To collect data on the survey questionnaire for these BCPs, following activities were carried out (Figure 18):

Figure 18: Key Activities Undertaken for Data Collation Under Cross-Border Trade and Transport Facilitation Index

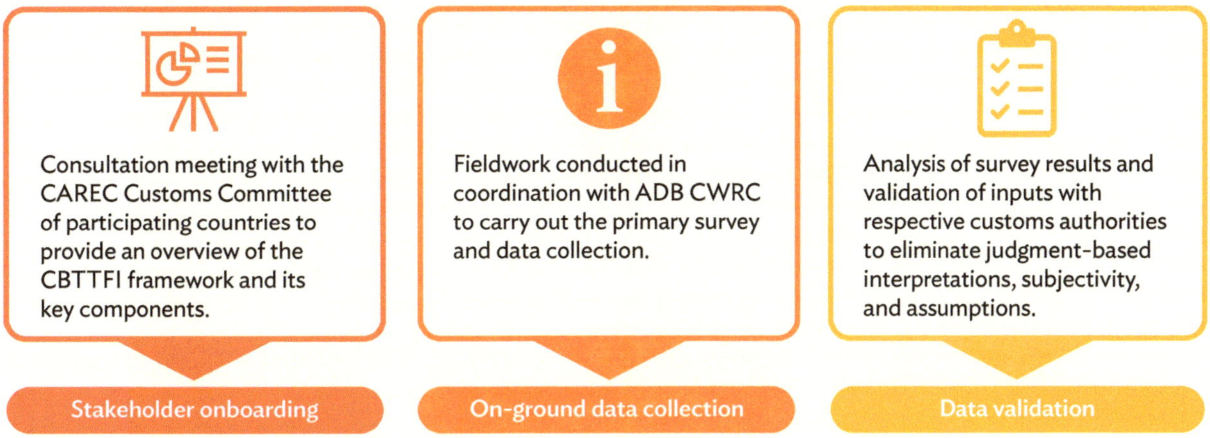

ADB = Asian Development Bank, CAREC = Central Asia Regional Economic Cooperation, CBTTFI = Cross-Border Trade and Transport Facilitation Index, CWRC = Regional Cooperation and Operations Coordination Division.

Source: Study team's approach.

Stakeholder onboarding: The stakeholder onboarding process aimed to ensure active participation and alignment among CAREC Customs Committee members regarding the CBTTFI framework. The consultation meeting served as a platform to introduce the index, explain its significance, and clarify expectations from participating countries.

On-ground data collection: This activity included primary data gathering through structured surveys with customs authorities and private sector stakeholders for identified BCPs, ensuring that the CBTTFI reflects ground realities.

Data validation: This activity included cross-verifying responses with customs authorities and eliminating subjective biases for ensuring the accuracy, reliability, and objectivity of collected data.

Assessment Methodology

The survey questionnaire contains 19 questions across the four trade and transport facilitation themes of the CBTTFI identified above, encompassing 100 marks as displayed in the Table 3.

Table 3: Questions and Scores by Theme

Theme Name	Total Questions	Total Score
Customs procedures and formalities	10	59
Customs coordination	3	13
Transit cross-border support facilities	4	26
Transport regulations	2	2
Total	**19**	**100**

Source: Cross-Border Trade and Transport Facilitation Index Survey Questionnaire (Annex 1).

To ensure consistency and balance across themes, a weighted scoring approach has been proposed for evaluating the CBTTFI (Table 4).

Table 4: Proposed Weight Range by Theme

Theme Name	Proposed Weight Range	Remarks
Customs procedures and formalities	50%–60%	It is one of the most critical components in cross-border trade facilitation, dealing with core issues such as document processing, clearance times, inspections, risk management, and automation. These processes have a direct impact on trade costs and delays. Further, this theme accounts for 59 out of 100 marks, i.e., 59% of the survey's total weight. Accordingly, a weight range of 50%–60% reflects both the quantitative share in the survey and the strategic importance in overall border efficiency.
Customs coordination	10%–15%	It covers important institutional aspects such as interagency cooperation, information sharing, and joint border controls. These are often critical enablers of efficiency, helping to reduce duplication and streamline procedures. Though not as visible as physical infrastructure or procedures, coordination plays a vital supporting role. Accordingly, a weight range of 10%–15% has been proposed.
Transit cross-border support facilities	20%–30%	Although it has fewer questions than Theme 1, this theme carries 26% of the marks, indicating substantial depth per question. It includes critical support infrastructure and services such as parking, warehousing, waiting areas, rest and relief services, which are essential for the smooth and humane functioning of transit across borders. These facilities enhance the quality and reliability of cross-border movement, particularly for time-sensitive and perishable goods. Hence, a 20%–30% weight range is proposed.
Transport regulations[a]	2%–5%	Transport regulations are necessary for safety and standardization, however, they have limited operational role at BCPs, as they are often set at a national level and enforced at those points. Accordingly, a 2%–5% weight range is proposed.

BCP = border crossing point.

[a] In assessing weight and dimension restrictions at BCPs, this report adopts a working assumption that the absence of such restrictions is favorable from a trade facilitation perspective. However, it is important to clarify that harmonization of restrictions across both sides of a BCP pair is more critical than the mere presence or absence of restrictions. If only one side of BCPs pair imposes weight or dimension constraints, or if thresholds differ significantly, this can result in delays, additional inspections, or even rerouting of cargo. Due to the unavailability of complete data for all counterpart BCPs, the current scoring reflects a single-sided view. However, where possible, bilateral harmonization needs to be prioritized.

Source: Study team's proposal under the Cross-Border Trade and Transport Facilitation Index framework.

For this study, a 55% weight has been considered for the theme customs procedures and formalities, 15% for customs coordination, 25% for transit and cross-border support, and 5% for transport regulations.

There are five types of scenarios for the questions in the survey for the CBTTFI and, depending on these scenarios, the responses for the questions are scored accordingly (Table 5).

Table 5: Survey Case Scenarios and Their Scoring Criteria

S. No.	Case Scenario	Scoring Type	Scoring Range	Scoring Criteria/Methodology
1	**Questions with response as "Yes"/"No"**	Binary	0 to 1 marks	**Unfavorable response:** 0 marks **Favorable response:** 1 mark
2	**Questions with graded case scenarios** *(response options ranging from unfavorable outcome to most favorable outcome)*	Likert scale approach	0 to 1 marks	**Unfavorable response:** 0 marks **Most favorable response:** 1 mark **Other graded favorable responses:** Proportionately increased from 0 to 1 marks
3	**Perception based questions**			
4	**Questions with numerical inputs:** (Utilization ratio, time efficiency index, operating hours %, TFI 1, and TFI 2)	Distance from frontier approach or range-based	0–8 marks	**Utilization ratio** (range-based): 0–2 marks **Operating hours %** (range-based): 0–2 marks[a] **Time efficiency index** (distance from frontier approach): 0–2 marks **TFI 1** (distance from frontier approach): 0–8 marks **TFI 2** (distance from frontier approach): 0–8 marks[b]
5	**Response type "Not applicable" to the respondent**	–	1 mark	NA score to be equivalent to most favorable response score (1 mark)

NA = not applicable, TFI = trade facilitation indicator.

[a] Range-based scoring has been adopted for calculating marks for utilization ratio parameter (>=0.75 and <=1.25: 2 marks; 0.5 to 0.75: 1 mark; 1.25 to 1.5: 1 mark; <0.5 or >1.5: 0 marks) and operating hours % parameter (100%: 2 marks; 80%–100%: 1.5 marks; 60%–80%: 1 mark; 30%–60%: 0.5 marks; <30%: 0 marks).

[b] Corridor Performance Measuring and Monitoring (CPMM) TFI 1 and TFI 2 have been assigned higher marks (8 each) in the Cross-Border Trade and Transport Facilitation Index survey because they offer a comprehensive and credible measure of the overall efficiency and cost-effectiveness of border procedures, capturing end-to-end trade facilitation performance. Unlike other infrastructure or operational metrics, these indicators reflect the real-time experience of traders, are sensitive to systemic inefficiencies, and are benchmarked using the Asian Development Bank's internationally recognized CPMM methodology. Their high weighting underscores their critical role in identifying bottlenecks, guiding policy reforms, and aligning with global trade facilitation standards focused on reducing time and cost at borders.

Source: Cross-Border Trade and Transport Facilitation Index Survey Questionnaire (Annex 1).

Box 3 details the numerical indexes included in the CBTTFI framework.

Box 3: Numerical Indexes Under Cross-Border Trade and Transport Facilitation Index Framework

There are five numerical indexes within the themes of the CBTTFI framework, developed to assess the operational performance of the border crossing points (BCPs) and guide policy improvements for increased efficiency. The following are the details for these indexes:

(i) **Utilization Ratio:** This ratio evaluates the extent to which a BCP's cargo-handling capacity is actively used over a month, providing a gauge of operational efficiency. A high utilization ratio indicates that the border point is operating near its maximum capacity, signaling efficient usage and potentially highlighting a need for expansion or resource scaling. Conversely, a low utilization ratio suggests underutilization, indicating a potential mismatch between capacity and demand. This index falls under the theme of transit and cross-border support facilities and is calculated using the formula:

Utilization ratio = (total number of loaded + empty trucks using the BCP per month)/(Maximum BCP cargo handling capacity per month)

continued on next page

Box 3 *continued*

(ii) **Time Efficiency Index:** This index measures the efficiency of time usage at the BCPs by assessing the processing time per truck relative to available operating hours. It helps gauge how effectively a BCP can handle traffic within its operational constraints. A higher Time Efficiency Index implies that the BCP is using its time and resources optimally to process goods, thus minimizing wait times and improving throughput. This metric is also included under the theme 'Transit and Cross-Border Support Facilities' and is calculated with the following formula:

*Time Efficiency Index = ([Total no. of trucks [loaded+empty] per month/30 days])/(no. of total lanes*BCP operating hrs)*

(iii) **Operating Hours (%):** This index evaluates the percentage of a 24-hour day that the BCP is operational, providing insight into synchronization with other BCPs for seamless cross-border movement. Higher synchronization scores reflect greater operational alignment with adjacent facilities, reducing delays in cross-border trade. This index is part of the 'Customs Coordination' theme and is calculated using the formula:

*Operating Hours % = (no. of operational hours of BCP per day/24 hours)*100%*

(iv) **CPMM TFI 1:** TFI 1 measures the time taken to clear customs at a BCP, highlighting delays and processing times that can affect the movement of goods. This forms part of the 'Customs Procedures and Formalities' theme of CBTTFI and its value is computed under CPMM analysis by ADB.

(v) **CPMM TFI 2:** TFI 2 calculates the cost incurred at a BCP, providing insight into the financial implications for trade facilitation. This also forms part of the 'Customs Procedures and Formalities' theme of CBTTFI and its value is computed under CPMM analysis by ADB.

ADB = Asian Development Bank, CBTTFI = Cross-Border Trade and Transport Facilitation Index, CPMM = corridor performance measurement and monitoring, TFI - trade facilitation indicator.
Source: Study team's proposal under the Cross-Border Trade and Transport Facilitation Index framework.

Based on the scoring methodology, the score of the CBTTFI for each border crossing point is calculated based on the below formula:

CBTTFI = Sum of score of BCP under each theme/(Total score – NA score of BCP).

The next section highlights case studies for the selected BCPs, showcasing the effectiveness of the CBTTFI in identifying the root causes for the bottlenecks at the BCPs and arrives at policy/regulatory, institutional, and infrastructural interventions required to address the bottlenecks and reduce the barriers to trade, thereby providing a platform for shared and sustainable development, in line with CAREC 2030 vision. This also serves as a base for continued performance evaluation for ADB projects and evidence-based policymaking.

Assessment of Selected Border Crossing Points on the Cross-Border Trade and Transport Facilitation Index

The following case studies assess performance of selected bordering crossings on the CBTTFI, highlighting their strengths and weaknesses.

Case Study 1: Kirmizi Korpu, Azerbaijan

Kirmizi Korpu BCP is in Gazakh, Azerbaijan on CAREC corridor no. 2 connecting Tbilisi, Georgia to Ganja, Azerbaijan. It features a red-brick arch bridge over the Khrami river, which marks the border. The crossing point has a maximum cargo handling capacity of 1,000 trucks per day with an expected annual traffic growth rate of 10% per year for the next 5 years. The border crossing has six dedicated lanes for truck examination operational 24/7.[10] The top-three cargo commodities passing the BCP include motor vehicles, tractors, and fresh/dried citrus fruits (footnote 10).

Kirmizi Korpu performs well across the different themes of the CBTTFI, securing a total weighted average score of 71%, as per the snapshot in Figure 19.

Figure 19: Performance of Kirmizi Korpu Border Crossing Point

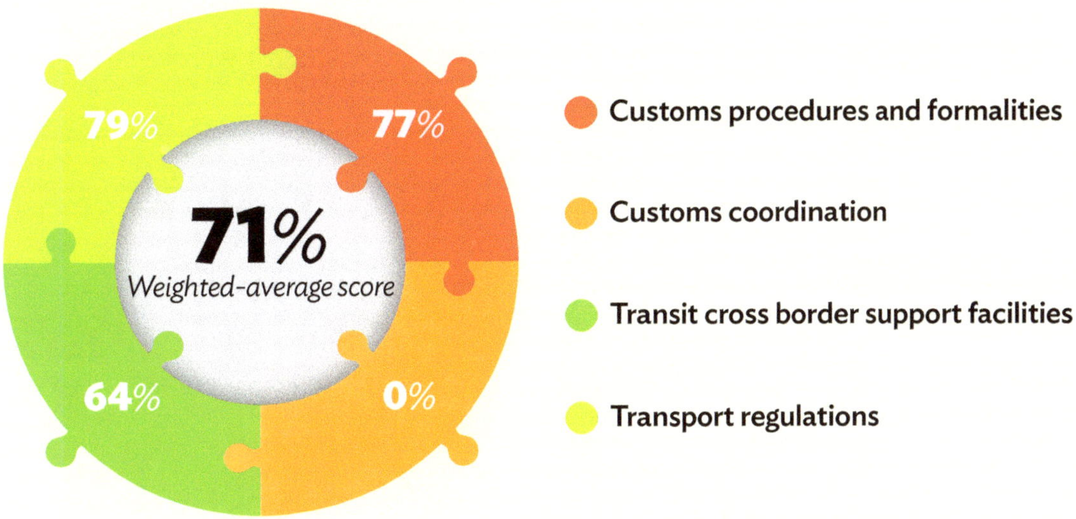

Source: Study team's calculations based on the Cross-Border Trade and Transport Facilitation Index survey.

[10] Questionnaire response from customs officials.

Customs procedures and formalities

The BCP scored 79% on this measure amid good practices such as electronic processing of various key documents such as packing list and/or cargo manifest, customs declaration and certificate of origin, among others (Figure 20). However, mandatory physical submission of original documents such as passport and/or national ID card, commercial driver's license, liability and cargo insurance, Transports Internationaux Routiers (TIR) carnet and/or customs bond at the BCP potentially increase the time taken for cargo vehicles to cross and may add cost.

The border point has most of the key ICT infrastructure in place, including an automated customs management system, electronic queue management systems, nonintrusive cargo inspection equipment, video surveillance systems, and e-TIR among others. There is also prior intimation given on (i) documentation requirements, (ii) testing and/or certification requirements, and (iii) inspection requirement after risk assessment. Further, pre-arrival clearance is also provided based on the submission of cargo manifest with requisite documents.

Figure 20: Performance of Kirmizi Korpu Border Crossing on Customs Procedures and Formalities

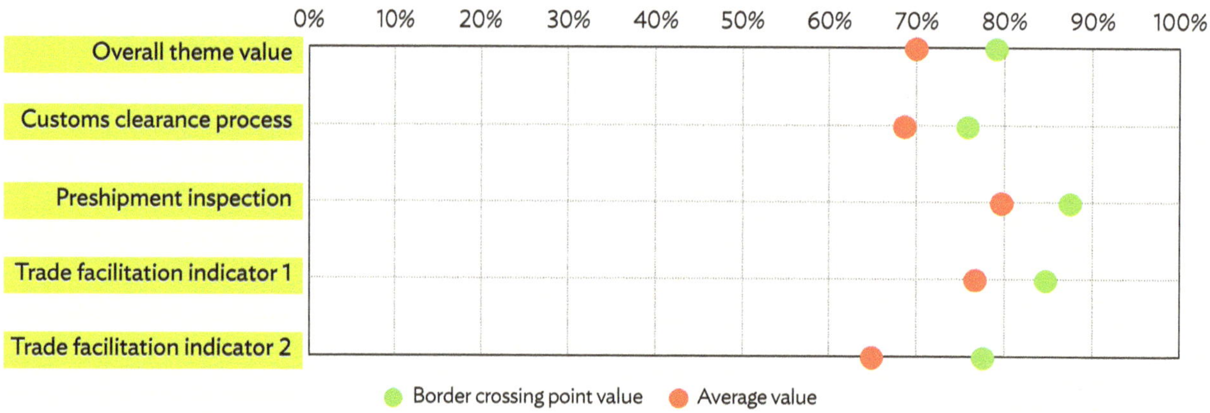

Note: "Average value" here refers to the average score for each parameter across the six shortlisted border crossing points.
Source: Study team's calculations based on the Cross-Border Trade and Transport Facilitation Index survey.

Physical inspection of goods at this BCP takes place only when necessitated by the computerized risk assessment system. Further, the BCP is equipped with sufficient staff for undertaking inspection, ensuring no delays take place in this process.

The customs valuation takes place based on World Trade Organization (WTO) Agreement for customs valuation and the customs classification is consistent in both headquarters and border, ensuring equal treatment across the different areas.

For the CPMM TFIs (2023), the time taken to cross a BCP is on the higher side, at 5.2 hours for inbound traffic (1.8 times higher than neighboring Tsiteli Khidi), while the cost incurred to cross the BCP is around $72, marginally lower than Tsiteli Khidi BCP. Based on "Distance to Frontier Approach," Kirmizi Korpu has attained the score 85% for time taken to cross the BCP and 78% for cost incurred, both of which are above the mean scores of 77% (time taken) and 65% (cost incurred), respectively (Figure 20).

Customs coordination

This BCP shows good performance with a score of 77% under this theme, indicating efficient cooperation mechanisms (Figure 21). Customs authorities report having provisions for joint control operations, including interoperable information systems and electronic data interchange between agencies. A data exchange agreement[11] between Azerbaijan and Georgia further supports the claim of cross-border data coordination. However, the actual extent of on-ground interoperability remains to be ascertained.

There is also provision for mutual recognition of documents including SPS and authorized economic operator certification, vehicle registration permits, customs guarantee for transport and cargo, driver's license, and insurance documents. These features easily enable the BCP to handle cargo capacity of up to 30,000 trucks per month (footnote 10). This BCP operates 24/7, in sync with its neighboring BCP, leading to higher coordination levels with the neighboring border point, thus scoring 100% on the synchronization index (Figure 21).

However, this BCP lacks synchronized clearance procedures with the neighboring BCP, and certificates such as inspection and quality certificates are not mutually recognized, resulting in slight delays.

Figure 21: Performance of Kirmizi Korpu Border Crossing Point on Customs Coordination

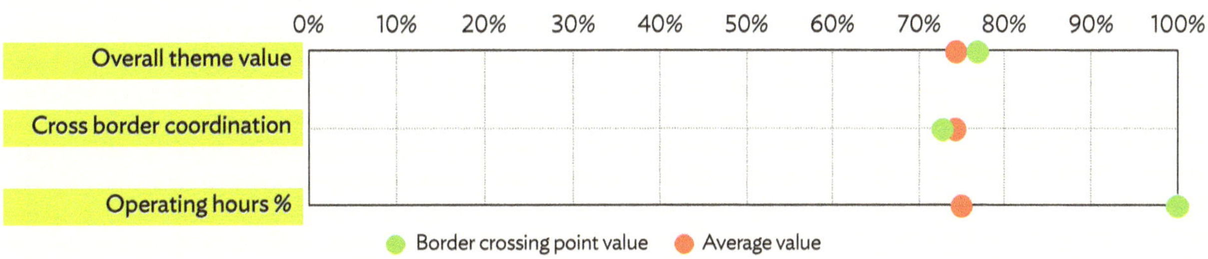

Note: "Average value" here refers to the average score for each parameter across the six shortlisted border crossing points.
Source: Study team's calculations based on the Cross-Border Trade and Transport Facilitation Index survey.

11 Implications of Single Window International Interoperability. https://www.carecprogram.org/uploads/Session-2_Yuebin-Zhang_SWII_ENG.pdf.

Transit cross-border support facilities

BCP scores 64% on this theme, with infrastructure facilities such as general and customs bonded warehouses, cargo transloading terminals, secure parking lots, maintenance-repair facilities, electric power generators and fuel stations at the premises of the BCP (Figure 22). Other facilities namely product testing laboratories, third-party inspection sites, quarantine treatment centers, emergency medical facilities and resting area for truck drivers are also available in the vicinity of the BCP area.

Figure 22: Performance of Kirmizi Korpu Border Crossing Point on Transit Cross-Border Support Facilities

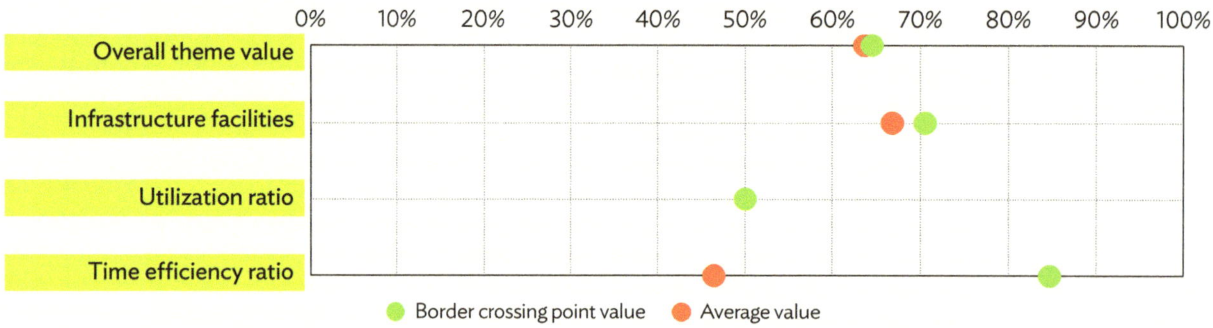

Note: "Average value" here refers to the average score for each parameter across the six shortlisted border crossing points.
Source: Study team's calculations based on the Cross-Border Trade and Transport Facilitation Index survey.

The utilization ratio for the BCP is currently 0.68 and is expected to increase further given that expected annual traffic growth rate is 10% per year. The time efficiency index for the BCP comes out as 4.7 trucks per lane per hour (translating to just 10% score against an average of 46% across the BCPs selected under the study, as shown in Figure 22), which clearly indicates that there is scope for improvement of the processing time per truck with the available resources. This also corroborates the fact that this BCP has the highest waiting/queuing time for inbound traffic, and second highest for outbound traffic at 4.1 hours and 15.8 hours, respectively as per the CPMM data captured in 2023.

Transport regulations

In light of transport regulations, there are weight and dimension limitations for cargo vehicles which are controlled by the Ministry of Transport, Communications and High Technologies. The permissible maximum height is 4 meters, width of 2.55 meters (2.60 meters for refrigerated vehicles), and maximum length of 12 meters for a lorry or trailer, with an articulated vehicle's maximum length up to 20 meters (OECD – International Transport Forum). The weight limit per single axle reaches 10 tons of cargo (OECD – International Transport Forum). These restrictions are mainly placed to regulate the traffic through the BCP which contains both passenger and freight vehicles. Due to these limitations, the BCP has not attained the desired score.

Table 6 presents key findings from the CBTTFI on the likely factors contributing to higher costs or delays across CPMM activities at the Kirmizi Korpu BCP.

Table 6: Kirmizi Korpu—Analysis of Corridor Performance Measurement and Monitoring Activities Based on Cross-Border Trade and Transport Facilitation Index Findings

S. No.	CPMM Activity	CPMM Value		Findings from CBTTFI Survey Attributing to Higher CPMM Value
		Time	Cost	
1	Border security and/or control	IN: 0.2 hrs OUT: 0.2 hrs	IN: $0 OUT: $0	• Mandatory physical submission of original documents for passport/ national card, commercial driver's license, vehicle registration document, certificate of liability insurance and TIR carnet/customs bond • Inadequate provisions for electronic application of customs refunds and e-CMR • Lack of provision to make advance fee payment for inspections • Absence of synchronized clearance procedures with the neighboring BCP
2	Customs controls	IN: 0.5 hrs OUT: 0.5 hrs	IN: $39 OUT: $32	
3	Commercial inspection	IN: - OUT: -	IN: - OUT: -	• Mutual recognition of inspection and quality certificates is not present currently • Product testing laboratories, facilities for third-party inspection and quarantine treatment centers are not available at the BCP, but only in its vicinity
4	Health and/or quarantine	IN: - OUT: -	IN: - OUT: -	
5	Phytosanitary	IN: - OUT: -	IN: - OUT: -	
6	Veterinary inspection	IN: 0.1 hrs OUT: -	IN: $0 OUT: -	
7	Visa and/or immigration	IN: - OUT: -	IN: - OUT: -	• Mandatory physical submission of passport and/or national ID card
8	Transit conformity	IN: 0.2 hrs OUT: -	IN: $0 OUT: -	• Computerized transit control system has only 50% service level up-time
9	GAI and/or traffic inspection	IN: - OUT: -	IN: - OUT: -	• Mandatory physical submission for Certificate of Liability Insurance • Computerized transit control systems, portable illegal drug identification systems with single window applications services are operational for only 50% of time
10	Police checkpoint or stop	IN: - OUT: -	IN: - OUT: -	• Mandatory physical submission for commercial driver's license
11	Transport inspection	IN: 0.1 hrs OUT: -	IN: $7 OUT: -	
12	Weight and/or standard inspection	IN: 0.1 hrs OUT: -	IN: $5 OUT: -	• There are weight and dimension limitations for cargo vehicles
13	Vehicle registration	IN: - OUT: -	IN: - OUT: -	• Mandatory physical submission for Vehicle Registration Document

continued on next page

Table 6 *continued*

S. No.	CPMM Activity	CPMM Value		Findings from CBTTFI Survey Attributing to Higher CPMM Value
		Time	Cost	
14	**Emergency repair**	IN: **-** OUT: **-**	IN: **-** OUT: **-**	• No gaps identified under the CBTTFI survey
15	**Escort or convoy**	IN: **-** OUT: **-**	IN: **-** OUT: **-**	• No gaps identified under the CBTTFI survey
16	**Loading and unloading**	IN: **-** OUT: **-**	IN: **-** OUT: **-**	• No gaps identified under the CBTTFI survey
17	**Road or bridge toll**	IN: **0.2 hrs** OUT: **0.2 hrs**	IN: **$26** OUT: **$25**	• No gaps identified under the CBTTFI survey
18	**Waiting or queueing**	IN: **4.1 hrs** OUT: **15.8 hrs**	IN: **$0** OUT: **$1**	• Electronic Queue Management Systems are available only for 80% up-time • The time efficiency index for the BCP comes out quite low at 4.7 trucks processed per lane per hour. • The utilization ratio for the BCP is 0.68 currently and is expected to increase further given that expected annual traffic growth rate is 10% per year.

BCP = border crossing point, CBTTFI = Cross-Border Trade and Transport Facilitation Index, CPMM = corridor performance measurement and monitoring, e-CMR = electronic consignment note, GAI = Gosudarstvennaya Avtomobilnaya Inspektsiya (State Automobile Inspectorate in Russian), IN = inbound traffic, OUT = outbound traffic, TIR = Transports Internationaux Routiers.

Source: Study team's findings based on the Cross-Border Trade and Transport Facilitation Index analysis.

Case Study 2: Tsiteli Khidi, Georgia

Tsiteli Khidi BCP is located in the province of Marneuli in Georgia (in the village of Kirach-Mughanlo) on CAREC corridor no. 2, connecting Tbilisi to Ganja, Azerbaijan. The border has maximum cargo handling capacity of nearly 985 trucks/containers per day with an expected annual traffic growth rate of 8%–10% per year for the next 5 years (footnote 10). The BCP has five lanes exclusively for truck examination, which are operational 24/7.

The top cargo commodities passing the BCP include petroleum, natural gas, and clinkers transported through freight vehicles which constitutes the traffic through the border (footnote 10).

Tsiteli Khidi performance is average, with a total weighted score of 64% across the various themes of the CBTTFI. Figure 23 presents the scores across the index themes.

Figure 23: Performance of Tsiteli Khidi Border Crossing Point

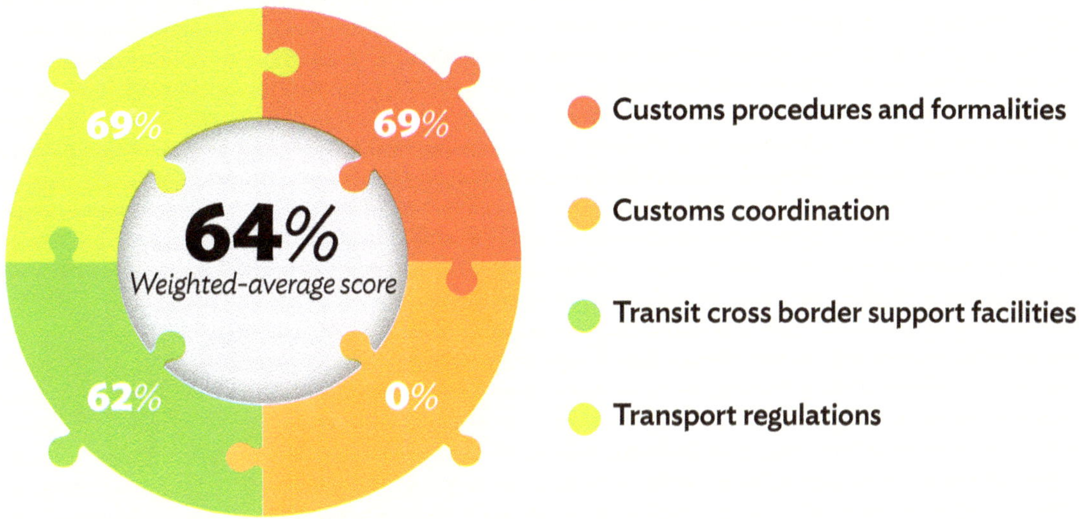

Source: Study team's calculations based on the Cross-Border Trade and Transport Facilitation Index survey.

Customs procedures and formalities

The BCP scored 69% on the customs procedures and formalities theme with the presence of good ICT infrastructure such as single window portal, automated customs management system, digital payment of customs duties and taxes, electronic queue management systems among other facilities which are available all time. There is also prior intimation on documentation requirements before testing and/or certification with the provision to make advance fee payment for inspections. Customs authorities process pre-arrival clearance based on submission of documents and electronic information exchange.

While the requirement for submission of original documents such as passport, visa, driver's license, vehicle registration, SPS certificate, and commercial invoice remains at many BCPs, the absence of digital pre-clearance mechanisms, or partial digitalization processes contributes to longer wait and queue times at these BCPs. Electronic pre-verification or submission of scanned copies ahead of arrival—followed by validation against originals helps expedite processing. Exploring similar digitalization practices, even within the constraints of mandatory original submission, could enhance efficiency without compromising regulatory compliance.

Further, the customs officials have overriding/discretionary powers to carry out physical inspections beyond the findings of computerized risk assessment algorithms which account for 5%–10% of physical inspection carried out. Accordingly, as shown in Figure 24, this BCP scores lower than the overall average score across customs clearance process and pre-shipment inspection subthemes under customs procedures and formalities.

With regard to the CPMM TFIs (2023), the time taken to cross Tsiteli Khidi is comparatively much lower than neighboring Kirmizi Korpu BCP, at 2.8 hours for inbound traffic, while the cost incurred to cross the border is around $97, higher than Kirmizi Korpu.

Figure 24: Performance of Tsiteli Khidi Border Crossing Point on Customs Procedures and Formalities

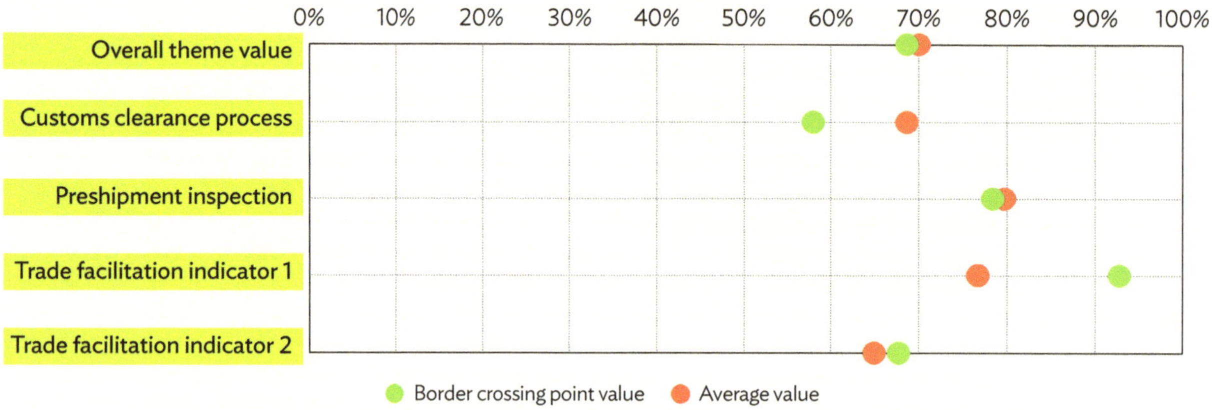

Note: "Average value" here refers to the average score for each parameter across the six shortlisted border crossing points.
Source: Study team's calculations based on the Cross-Border Trade and Transport Facilitation Index survey.

Customs coordination

Tsiteli Khidi BCP scored 69% on the customs coordination theme (Figure 25) with the mechanism for electronic data interchange between customs authorities to aid the joint control operations. A data exchange agreement between Azerbaijan and Georgia further supports the claim of cross-border data coordination (footnote 11). There are also provisions for mutual recognition of documents, including inspection and SPS certificates, vehicle registration documents and/or permits, customs guarantee for transport and cargo, driver's license, and quality certifications.

However, border and customs controls are currently applied separately at each side of the border crossing and cross-border coordination is therefore limited. The border point could take steps to introduce synchronized cross-border clearance procedures and interoperable information systems between customs authorities for faster clearance. Provisions could also be created for the mutual recognition of authorized economic operator certification and insurance documents.

The border point operates 24 hours a day in synchronization with neighboring Kirmizi Korpu to effectively process around 29,550 maximum cargo trucks a month (footnote 10).

Figure 25: Performance of Tsiteli Khidi Border Crossing on Customs Coordination

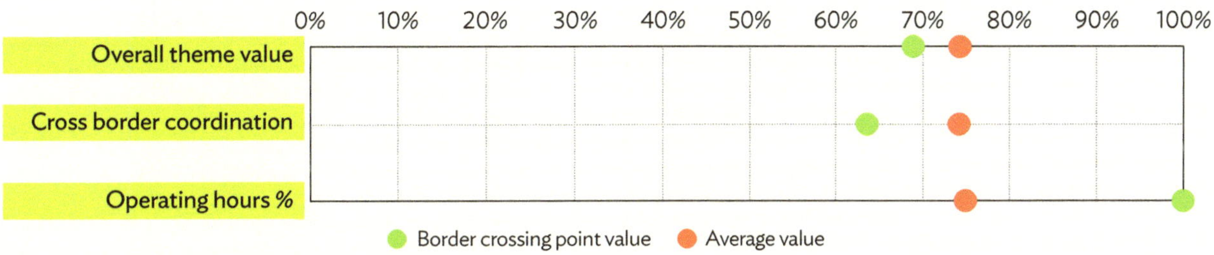

Note: "Average value" here refers to the average score for each parameter across the six shortlisted border crossing points.
Source: Study team's calculations based on the Cross-Border Trade and Transport Facilitation Index survey.

Transit cross-border support facilities

In this area, the BCP scored 62%, which is closer to the average score of 64% among the border crossings selected for the analysis (Figure 26). Logistics infrastructure such as general storage/customs bonded warehouses, cargo transloading terminals, secure vehicle parking lots, maintenance repair facilities for cargo vehicles, and fueling stations are present in the vicinity of border crossing. At the border crossing, quarantine treatment centers, electric power generators, banking facilities, and insurance agencies are available to provide the required support for transit trucks. Additionally, introduction is ongoing of an extra transport lane for trucks to meet an expected traffic increase of 8%–10% per year for the next 5 years (footnote 10).

Figure 26: Performance of Tsiteli Khidi Border Crossing on Transit Cross-Border Support Facilities

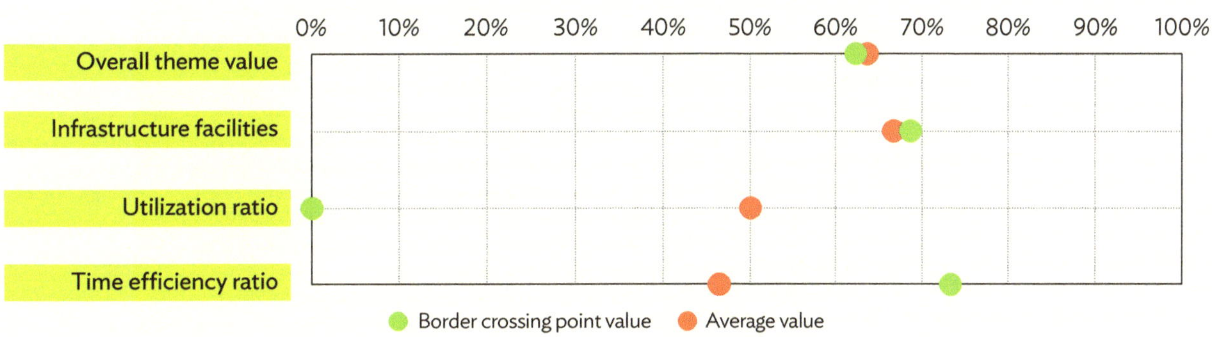

Note: "Average value" here refers to the average score for each parameter across the six shortlisted border crossing points.
Source: Study team's calculations based on the Cross-Border Trade and Transport Facilitation Index survey.

The utilization ratio for the BCP is as high as 1.85 and is expected to increase further given anticipated annual traffic growth of 10% per year. This significantly high utilization ratio indicates that the BCP is operating beyond its maximum capacity, signaling the need for expansion or resource scaling. Accordingly, it fares very poorly in comparison to the other border crossings on this front.

However, the time efficiency index for the BCP comes out as 15.2 trucks per lane per hour, indicating no delay in the processing of customs cargo trucks.

Transport regulations

In this area, weight and dimension limitations exist for cargo vehicles, which are mandated by the Government of Georgia Resolution No.393 of 11 August 2017 in Tbilisi. In Georgia, the legal weight and dimension limits for cargo vehicles are 80,000 pounds, 13 feet 6 inches high, 8 feet 6 inches wide, and 100 feet long (including overhang).[12] Vehicles exceeding these limits require special transit permits.[13] These restrictions are mainly placed to regulate the traffic through the border point, which contains only freight vehicles. The BCP has scored low on this theme, well below the average score of 42% among the selected BCPs, mainly due to the weight and dimension limitations.

Table 7 presents the key findings from the CBTTFI on the likely factors contributing to higher costs or delays across CPMM activities at the Tsiteli Khidi BCP.

Table 7: Tsiteli Khidi—Analysis of Corridor Performance Measurement and Monitoring Activities Based on Cross-Border Trade and Transport Facilitation Index Findings

S. No.	CPMM Activity	CPMM Value		Findings from CBTTFI Survey Attributing to Higher CPMM Value
		Time	Cost	
1	**Border security and/or control**	IN: **0.0 hrs** OUT: **0.0 hrs**	IN: **$0** OUT: **$0**	• Mandatory physical submission of original documents for passport and/or national card, visa, commercial driver's license, permit for vehicle entry, vehicle registration document, certificate of liability insurance, TIR carnet/customs bond, CMR consignment note, SPS certificate and commercial invoice • Lack of prior intimation of inspection requirement upon risk assessment • Officials have overriding and/or discretionary powers to carry out physical inspections beyond findings of computerized risk assessment algorithms which account for 5%–10% inspection • Lack of synchronized clearance procedures with the neighboring BCP and interoperable information systems between customs authorities
2	**Customs controls**	IN: **0.0 hrs** OUT: **0.0 hrs**	IN: **$0** OUT: **$0**	

continued on next page

12 Georgia Department of Public Safety - Permits for Vehicles or loads of excess weight or dimension.
13 Georgia Department of Transportation - Oversize Permits.

Table 7 *continued*

S. No.	CPMM Activity	CPMM Value: Time	CPMM Value: Cost	Findings from CBTTFI Survey Attributing to Higher CPMM Value
3	**Commercial inspection**	IN: –	IN: –	• Mutual recognition of AEO certification and insurance documents is not present currently
		OUT: –	OUT: –	
4	**Health and/or quarantine**	IN: –	IN: –	
		OUT: –	OUT: –	
5	**Phytosanitary**	IN: –	IN: –	
		OUT: –	OUT: –	
6	**Veterinary inspection**	IN: –	IN: –	
		OUT: –	OUT: –	
7	**Visa and/or immigration**	IN: –	IN: –	• Mandatory physical submission of passport and/or national ID card
		OUT: –	OUT: –	
8	**Transit conformity**	IN: –	IN: –	• No gaps identified under the CBTTFI survey
		OUT: –	OUT: –	
9	**GAI and/or traffic inspection**	IN: –	IN: –	• Mandatory physical submission for Certificate of Liability Insurance and Cargo Insurance
		OUT: –	OUT: –	
10	**Police checkpoint or stop**	IN: –	IN: –	• Mandatory physical submission for commercial driver's license • Officials have overriding/discretionary powers to carry out physical inspections beyond findings of computerized risk assessment algorithms which account for 5%–10% inspection
		OUT: –	OUT: –	
11	**Transport inspection**	IN: **0.0 hrs**	IN: **$0**	
		OUT: –	OUT: –	
12	**Weight and/or standard inspection**	IN: –	IN: –	• There are weight and dimension limitations for cargo vehicles
		OUT: –	OUT: –	
13	**Vehicle registration**	IN: –	IN: –	• Mandatory physical submission for Vehicle Registration Document and Permit for Vehicle entry
		OUT: –	OUT: –	
14	**Emergency repair**	IN: –	IN: –	• Maintenance repair facilities for vehicles are available only in the vicinity of BCP which could be developed at the BCP
		OUT: –	OUT: –	
15	**Escort or convoy**	IN: –	IN: –	• No gaps identified under the CBTTFI survey
		OUT: –	OUT: –	
16	**Loading and unloading**	IN: –	IN: –	• Cargo transloading terminals are available only in the vicinity of BCP which could be developed at the BCP
		OUT: –	OUT: –	
17	**Road or bridge toll**	IN: **0.1 hrs**	IN: **$134**	• The toll costs are high compared to the average value of $97
		OUT: **0.1 hrs**	OUT: **$133**	
18	**Waiting or queueing**	IN: **2.6 hrs**	IN: **$0**	• The utilization ratio is very high and is expected to increase further given that expected annual traffic growth rate is 8%–10% per year
		OUT: **54.7 hrs**	OUT: **$34**	

AEO = authorized economic operator, BCP = border crossing point, CPMM = corridor performance measurement and monitoring, CBTTFI = Cross-Border Trade and Transport Facilitation Index, CMR = Convention on the Contract for the International Carriage of Goods by Road, GAI = Gosudarstvennaya Avtomobilnaya Inspektsiya (State Automobile Inspectorate in Russian), IN = inbound traffic, OUT = outbound traffic, SPS = sanitary and phytosanitary, TIR = Transports Internationaux Routiers.

Source: Study team's findings based on the Cross-Border Trade and Transport Facilitation Index analysis.

Case Study 3: Serhetabat, Turkmenistan

Serhetabat BCP is in Mary Velayat Province in Turkmenistan on CAREC corridors 2 and 6, connecting Turkmenistan with Afghanistan. The BCP has a maximum cargo handling capacity of 5,700 trucks per month with only a single lane in place for cargo vehicles (footnote 10). Nearly 90 to 100 are incoming and outgoing and inspected daily at the border crossing, with traffic volume over the next 5 years projected to grow 5%–10% annually (footnote 10).

The top-three commodities passing through this border are liquefied gas and petroleum products, mineral fertilizers, and industrial/household goods, with peak months in January, February, and September to December. The crossing point is then operational 9 hours daily: 9 a.m. to 6 p.m.

Serhetabat BCP scores 60% across the themes of the CBTTFI, with scores across the themes in Figure 27.

Figure 27: Performance of Serhetabat Border Crossing Point

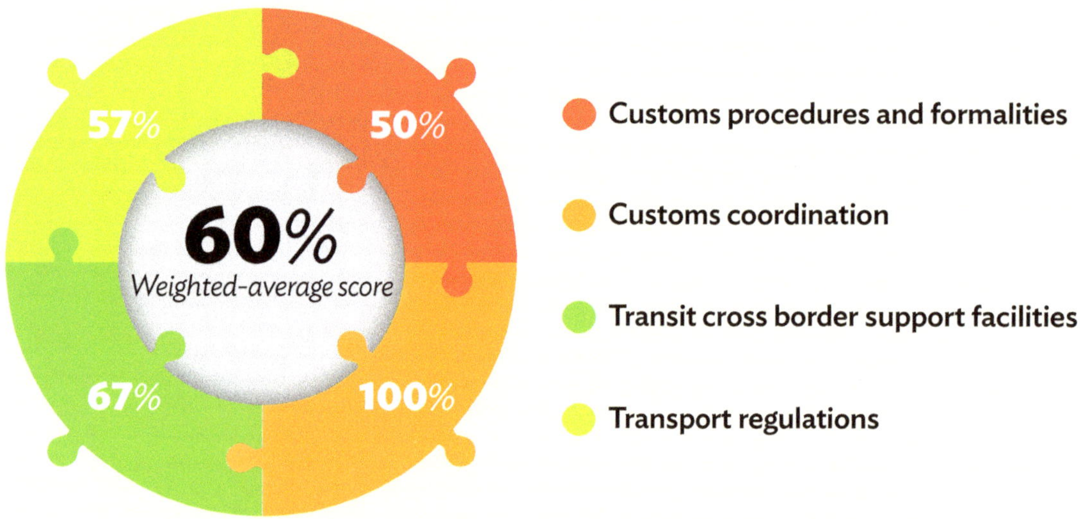

Source: Study team's calculations based on the Cross-Border Trade and Transport Facilitation Index survey.

Customs procedures and formalities

The BCP performs well in this area, with the required customs ICT infrastructure in place, such as single window portal, automated customs management system, nonintrusive inspection equipment, computerized transit and automated passport control systems, video surveillance with automatic radiation detection mechanisms, portable illegal drug identification systems, and an automated system for SPS inspection/declarations. There is also prior intimation of an inspection requirement upon risk assessment and provision to make advance fee payment for inspections to expedite the process. With sufficient customs officials, physical inspection only takes place based on feedback from risk assessment algorithms, which accounts for 5%–10% inspection.

Customs valuation takes place based on WTO agreement and customs classification is consistent among customs headquarters and borders to ensure uniformity. However, while submission of original documents such as passport, visa, commercial driver's license, permit for vehicle entry, and customs bond is a standard requirement across BCPs, the current process lacks provisions for electronic pre-submission or digital pre-clearance of these documents. Further, ICT systems such as electronic payment and/or digital payment of duties and taxes, application for customs refunds, queue management systems, e-TIR and e-CMR—including provision for prior intimation on testing and/or certification requirements—are not now available at the BCP. Due to these constraints, the border crossing has scored 57%, below the overall average 70% on the customs procedures and formalities theme (Figure 28). The scores of subthemes such as customs clearance process and pre-shipment inspection is also behind mean scores.

Considering CPMM TFIs, the time taken to cross the border is the least, at 0.7 hours (2022) for inbound traffic (nearly 4.8 hours less than another BCP—Farap in Turkmenistan). Data showing cost incurred to cross the border is not available for the latest year and hence it is not considered (Figure 28).

Figure 28: Performance of Serhetabat Border Crossing Point on Customs Procedures and Formalities

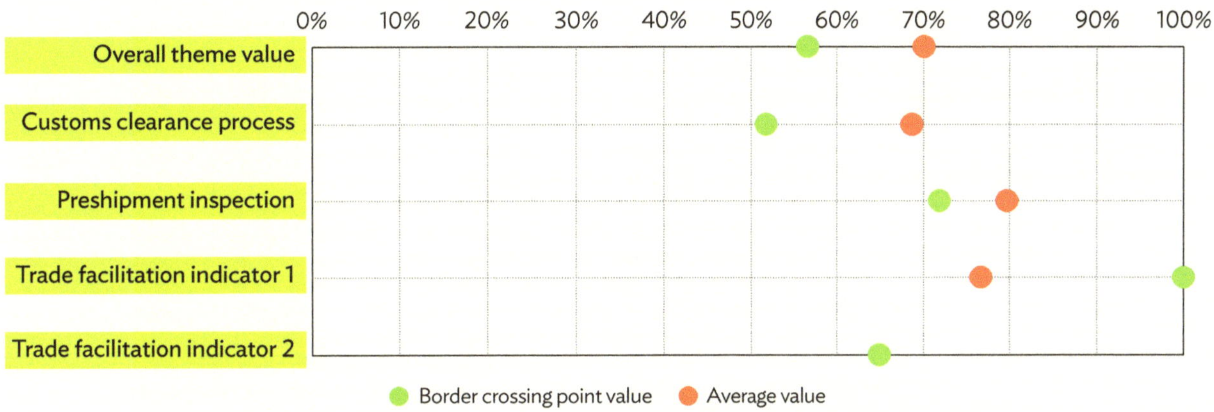

Note: "Average value" here refers to the average score for each parameter across the six shortlisted border crossing points.
Source: Study team's calculations based on the Cross-Border Trade and Transport Facilitation Index survey.

Customs coordination

In this area, the border BCP scored 50%, below the comparative average score of 74% among other BCPs analyzed in the study (Figure 29). Customs authorities report having provisions of electronic cross-border data exchange between customs authorities, though the on-ground implementation of the same is yet to be ascertained. Mutual recognition of documents including vehicle registration permits, customs guarantee for transport and cargo, driver's license, insurance documents, and quality certifications are currently in practice at the BCP. However, provisions are lacking for mutual recognition of authorized economic operator certificates, SPS certificates, and inspection certificates, along with availability of interoperable information systems between customs authorities and synchronized clearance procedures.

Further, since the BCP is operating only for 9 hours a day, the value of "operating hours %" indicator comes as only 25%, much below the average value of 75% compared to other BCPs (Figure 29).

Figure 29: Performance of Serhetabat Border Crossing Point on Customs Coordination

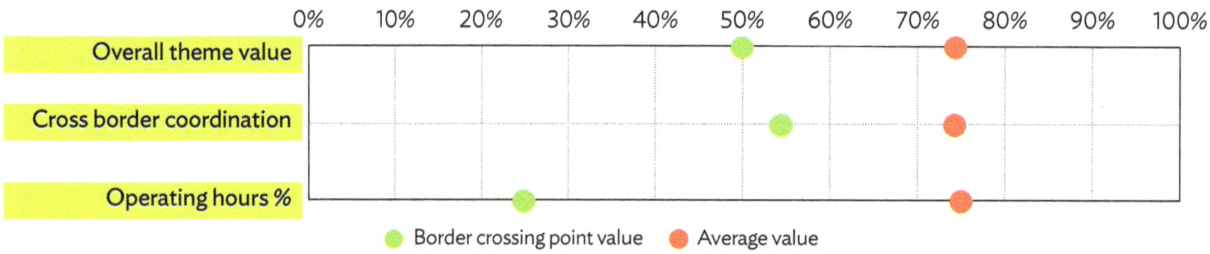

Note: "Average value" here refers to the average score for each parameter across the six shortlisted border crossing points.
Source: Study team's calculations based on the Cross-Border Trade and Transport Facilitation Index survey.

Transit cross-border support facilities

The BCP performs well in transit cross-border support facilities, with an overall score of 67% (Figure 30). Electric power generators, banking solutions, and emergency medical facilities are conveniently present at the BCP location. However, most of the logistics and testing infrastructure such as general storage/customs bonded warehouses, cargo transloading terminals, logistics hubs, fueling stations, quarantine treatment centers, facilities for third-party inspection, and material handling equipment for heavy cargo processing are available only in the vicinity of the BCP. Thus, the score under infrastructure facilities subtheme is 61%, i.e., below the average score of 67%.

The utilization ratio for the BCP is 0.93 currently, indicating high operational efficiency of cargo-handling capacity. Accordingly, this BCP scores 100% for the "utilization ratio" indicator (Figure 30).

Figure 30: Performance of Serhetabat Border Crossing Point on Transit Cross-Border Support Facilities

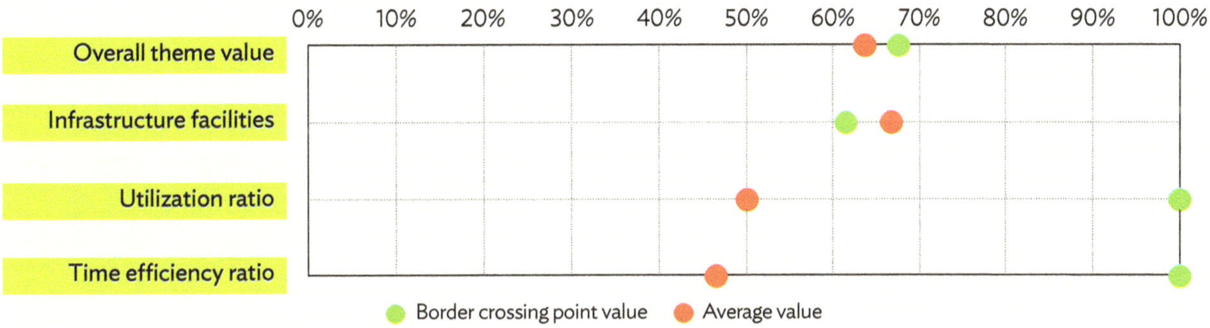

Note: "Average value" here refers to the average score for each parameter across the six shortlisted border crossing points.
Source: Study team's calculations based on the Cross-Border Trade and Transport Facilitation Index survey.

The time efficiency index for the BCP comes out as 19.6 trucks per lane per hour, showing that the processing of customs cargo trucks is fastest among the BCPs, and it thus scores 100% on this indicator.

Transport regulations

The BCP has scored 100% on the transport regulations theme, with no weight and dimension limitations for cargo vehicles. This may be beneficial for large-scale imports and exports, helping businesses avoid bottlenecks and ensuring shipments are delivered on time.

Table 8 presents key findings from the CBTTFI on the likely factors contributing to higher costs or delays across CPMM activities at the Serhetabat BCP.

Table 8: Serhetabat—Analysis of Corridor Performance Measurement and Monitoring Activities Based on Cross-Border Trade and Transport Facilitation Index Findings

S. No.	CPMM Activity	Findings from CBTTFI Survey Attributing to Higher CPMM Value
1	Border security and/or control	• Mandatory physical submission of original documents for passport and/or national card, visa, commercial driver's license, permit for vehicle entry, vehicle registration document, TIR carnet/Customs bond, CMR consignment note, cargo manifest and commercial invoice • Lack of prior intimation on testing and/or certification requirements and pre-arrival clearance • Lack of synchronized clearance procedures with the neighboring BCP and interoperable information systems between customs authorities
2	Customs controls	
3	Commercial inspection	• Mutual recognition of AEO certification and inspection and/or SPS certifications are not present currently • Lack of prior intimation on testing and/or certification requirements
4	Health and/or quarantine	
5	Phytosanitary	
6	Veterinary inspection	
7	Visa and/or immigration	• Mandatory physical submission of passport/national ID card
8	Transit conformity	• No gaps identified under the CBTTFI survey

continued on next page

Table 8 *continued*

S. No.	CPMM Activity	Findings from CBTTFI Survey Attributing to Higher CPMM Value
9	GAI and/or traffic inspection	• No gaps identified under the CBTTFI survey
10	Police checkpoint or stop	• Mandatory physical submission for commercial driver's license
11	Transport inspection	
12	Weight and/or standard inspection	• No gaps identified under the CBTTFI survey
13	Vehicle registration	• Mandatory physical submission for Vehicle Registration Document and Permit for Vehicle entry
14	Emergency repair	• Maintenance repair facilities for vehicles are available only in the vicinity of BCP which could be developed at the BCP
15	Escort or convoy	• No gaps identified under the CBTTFI survey
16	Loading and unloading	• Cargo transloading terminals are available only in the vicinity of BCP which could be developed at the BCP
17	Road or bridge toll	• No gaps identified under the CBTTFI survey
18	Waiting or queueing	• Only a single lane in place for cargo vehicles

AEO = authorized economic operator, BCP = border crossing point, CBTTFI = Cross-Border Trade and Transport Facilitation Index, CMR = Convention on the Contract for the International Carriage of Goods by Road, CPMM = corridor performance measurement and monitoring, GAI = Gosudarstvennaya Avtomobilnaya Inspektsiya (State Automobile Inspectorate in Russian) SPS = sanitary and phytosanitary, TIR = Transports Internationaux Routiers.

Source: Study team's findings based on the Cross-Border Trade and Transport Facilitation Index analysis.

Case Study 4: Farap, Turkmenistan

Farap BCP is located in Lebap Velayat region of Turkmenistan which is situated on the CAREC corridors 2 and 3 and considered a major border crossing connecting the city of Farap, Turkmenistan with the city of Alat, Uzbekistan . There are four lanes in the BCP which are utilized exclusively for freight vehicles (operational for 24 hours), with the maximum cargo handling capacity for the BCP being 800 trucks/containers per day (footnote 10). The expected annual traffic growth rate is 20% for the next 5 years.

The top-three commodities passing through this BCP are cotton yarn, dried fruits, and mineral fertilizers.

Farap BCP attained a total weighted average score of 59% across the various themes of the CBTTFI which is below the overall average score 68%. Figure 31 is a snapshot of the total score of the index and individual scores across the different themes.

Figure 31: Performance of Farap Border Crossing Point

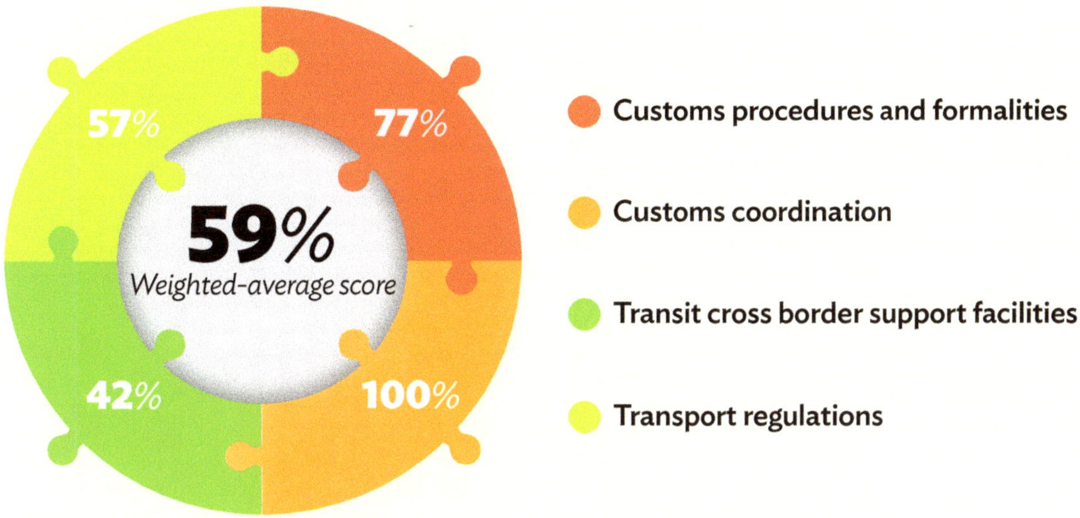

Source: Study team's calculations based on the Cross-Border Trade and Transport Facilitation Index survey.

Customs procedures and formalities

Farap BCP has ICT infrastructure for customs processing such as automated customs management system, nonintrusive cargo inspection, computerized transit control systems, video surveillance, automatic radiation detection, and automated mechanism for SPS inspection and/or declarations. There is also prior intimation of inspection requirement upon risk assessment and advance fee payment process for inspections. The risk management is robust, thus only less than 5% physical inspection takes place based on the results from feedback of the assessment system.

Although there is advanced ICT infrastructure, most of the required documents are not uploaded and processed electronically. While mandatory physical submission of original documents such as passport, visa, commercial driver's license, permit for vehicle entry, customs bond, cargo manifest, and customs declaration are a standard requirement across most BCPs, the absence of digital presubmission or pre-arrival processing mechanisms results in manual handling and contributes to delays. Due to current manual processes, the border crossing has scored 57% under this theme (Figure 32). Further, ICT infrastructure such as digital payment of duties/taxes, electronic queue management and application for customs refunds with e-TIR and e-CMR are not present at the border crossing, leading to a low score of 40% under the customs clearance process subtheme (Figure 32).

By CPMM TFI (2023), the time taken to cross the BCP is quite high among the selected BCPs, at 5.5 hours for inbound traffic, nearly 4.8 hours more than Serhetabat BCP in Turkmenistan. The cost incurred to cross the border is around $70, translating to a score of 84% and 78% on TFIs 1 and 2, respectively, higher than the average values across the selected BCPs.

Figure 32: Performance of Farap Border Crossing Point on Customs Procedures and Formalities

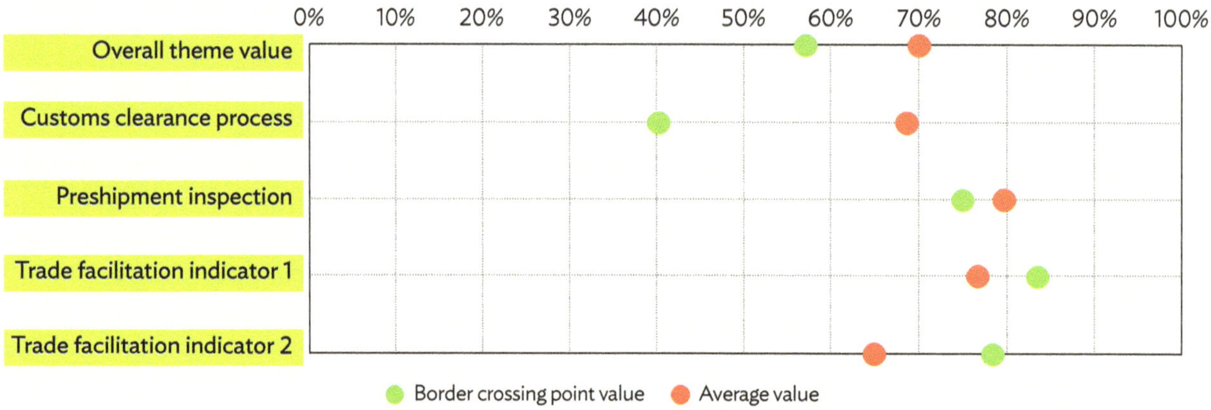

Note: "Average value" here refers to the average score for each parameter across the six shortlisted border crossing points.
Source: Study team's calculations based on the Cross-Border Trade and Transport Facilitation Index survey.

Customs coordination

Farap BCP secured 77% under the customs coordination theme, faring slightly better than the overall average score of 74% for the analyzed BCPs (Figure 33). Customs authorities report having provisions of joint customs control operations such as synchronized clearance procedures, interoperable information systems, and electronic data interchange between customs authorities. However, the actual extent of on-ground implementation of the same remains to be ascertained. Further, mutual recognition of documents including vehicle registration permits, driver's license, insurance documents, quality certifications and customs guarantee for transport/cargo are also provided in the BCP.

The BCP is operational 24 hours a day, effectively processing around 24,000 maximum cargo trucks in a month (Figure 33) (footnote 10).

Figure 33: Performance of Farap Border Crossing Point on Customs Coordination

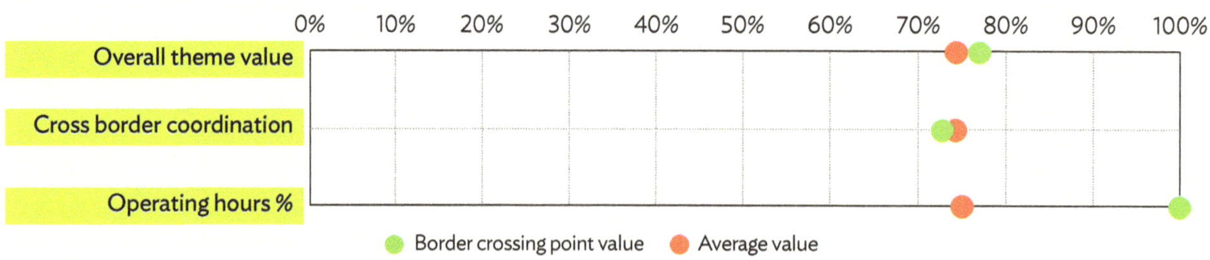

Note: "Average value" here refers to the average score for each parameter across the six shortlisted border crossing points.
Source: Study team's calculations based on the Cross-Border Trade and Transport Facilitation Index survey.

Transit cross-border support facilities

Logistical infrastructure facilities such as customs bonded warehouses, fueling stations, parking space, maintenance—repair provisions for vehicles, product testing labs, third-party inspection area, quarantine treatment centers, and material handling equipment for heavy cargo are available only in the vicinity of the BCP while cargo transloading terminals, electric power generators, and banking facilities are provided at the BCP locality. The BCP attained an overall score of 42% which is lesser than the average score of 64% (Figure 34).

The utilization ratio for the BCP is currently 0.36, indicating underutilization of the border crossing, and therefore highlighting a potential mismatch between capacity and demand. This has led to the border point scoring 0% score as against the average value of 50% for the selected border crossings under study.

The time efficiency index for the border crossing comes out as three trucks per lane per hour, which clearly indicates that there is scope for improvement of the processing time per truck with the available resources. As a result, this BCP scored 0% on this indicator as well, as shown in Figure 34.

Figure 34: Performance of Farap Border Crossing Point on Transit Cross-Border Support Facilities

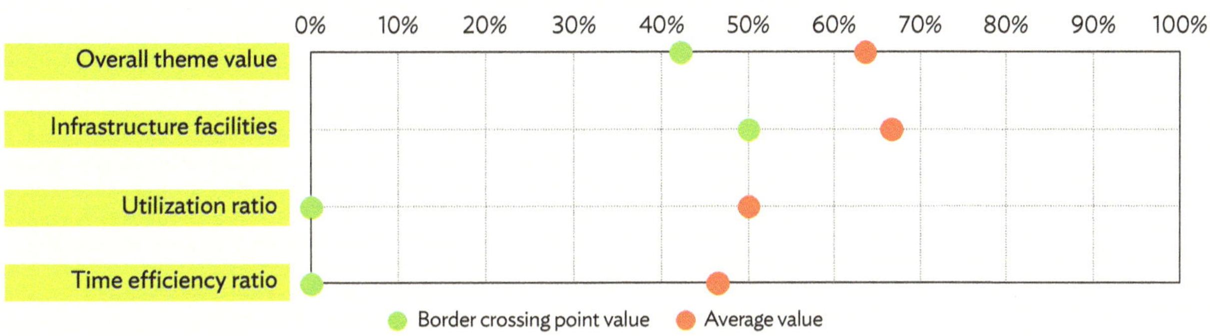

Note: "Average value" here refers to the average score for each parameter across the six shortlisted border crossing points.
Source: Study team's calculations based on the Cross-Border Trade and Transport Facilitation Index survey.

Transport regulations

Similar to Serhetabat BCP, the Farap border crossing also scored 100% in the transport regulations, with no weight and dimension limitation for cargo vehicles.

Table 9 presents the key findings from the CBTTFI on the likely factors contributing to higher costs or delays across CPMM activities at Farap.

Table 9: Farap—Analysis of Corridor Performance Measurement and Monitoring Activities Based on Cross-Border Trade and Transport Facilitation Index Findings

S. No.	CPMM Activity	CPMM Value		Findings from CBTTFI Survey Attributing to Higher CPMM Value
		Time	Cost	
1	Border security and/or control	IN: 0.1 hrs OUT: –	IN: – OUT: –	• Mandatory physical submission of original documents for passport and/or national card, visa, commercial driver's license, permit for vehicle entry, vehicle registration document, TIR carnet/Customs bond, CMR consignment note, cargo manifest, customs declaration and commercial invoice • Inadequate provision for digital payment of duties and taxes, electronic queue management systems and electronic application for customs refunds • Lack of prior intimation on testing and/or certification requirements
2	Customs controls	IN: 0.2 hrs OUT: –	IN: – OUT: –	
3	Commercial inspection	IN: – OUT: –	IN: – OUT: –	• Mutual recognition of inspection and/or SPS certificates and AEO certification is not present currently
4	Health and/or quarantine	IN: 0.1 hrs OUT: –	IN: – OUT: –	
5	Phytosanitary	IN: – OUT: –	IN: – OUT: –	
6	Veterinary inspection	IN: – OUT: –	IN: – OUT: –	
7	Visa and/or immigration	IN: – OUT: –	IN: – OUT: –	• Mandatory physical submission of passport/national ID card
8	Transit conformity	IN: – OUT: –	IN: – OUT: –	• No gaps identified under the CBTTFI survey
9	GAI and/or traffic inspection	IN: – OUT: –	IN: – OUT: –	• No gaps identified under the CBTTFI survey
10	Police checkpoint or stop	IN: – OUT: –	IN: – OUT: –	• Mandatory physical submission for commercial driver's license
11	Transport inspection	IN: 0.2 hrs OUT: –	IN: – OUT: –	
12	Weight and/or standard inspection	IN: 0.2 hrs OUT: –	IN: – OUT: –	• No gaps identified under the CBTTFI survey
13	Vehicle registration	IN: – OUT: –	IN: – OUT: –	• Mandatory physical submission for vehicle registration document and permit for vehicle entry
14	Emergency repair	IN: – OUT: –	IN: – OUT: –	• Maintenance repair facilities for vehicles are available only in the vicinity of BCP which could be developed at the BCP
15	Escort or convoy	IN: – OUT: –	IN: – OUT: –	• No gaps identified under the CBTTFI survey
16	Loading and unloading	IN: 1.8 hrs OUT: –	IN: – OUT: –	• No gaps identified under the CBTTFI survey
17	Road or bridge toll	IN: 0.4 hrs OUT: –	IN: $70 OUT: –	• No gaps identified under the CBTTFI survey

continued on next page

Table 9 *continued*

S. No.	CPMM Activity	CPMM Value		Findings from CBTTFI Survey Attributing to Higher CPMM Value
		Time	Cost	
18	**Waiting or queueing**	IN: **2.6 hrs** OUT: -	IN: - OUT: -	• In spite of low utilization ratio, the time efficiency index for the BCP is 3 trucks per lane per hour, which clearly indicates that there is scope for improvement of the processing time per truck with the available resources.

AEO = authorized economic operator, BCP = border crossing point, CBTTFI = Cross-Border Trade and Transport Facilitation Index, CMR = Convention on the Contract for the International Carriage of Goods by Road, CPMM = corridor performance measurement and monitoring, GAI = Gosudarstvennaya Avtomobilnaya Inspektsiya (State Automobile Inspectorate in Russian), IN = inbound traffic, OUT = outbound traffic, SPS = sanitary and phytosanitary, TIR = Transports Internationaux Routiers.

Source: Study team's findings based on the Cross-Border Trade and Transport Facilitation Index analysis.

Case Study 5: Torkham, Pakistan

Torkham BCP is located in Khyber Pakhtunkhwa province of Peshawar City of Pakistan on CAREC corridors 5 and 6, connecting to Nangarhar Province of Afghanistan. The border point has 12 lanes used exclusively for truck examination. The maximum cargo handling capacity of the border point is 72,000 trucks/containers in a month. It is operational 9 hours (daytime) in coordination with the neighboring BCP (footnote 10). Annual traffic growth is expected to be 20% per year for the next 5 years (footnote 10).

Sugar, cooking oil, and soybeans are the top-three cargo commodities passing through this BCP and the peak months for cross border passage are April to October.

Torkham scored total weighted average of 75% across the various themes of the CBTTFI. Figure 35 presents a snapshot of the total score on the different themes.

Figure 35: Performance of Torkham Border Crossing Point

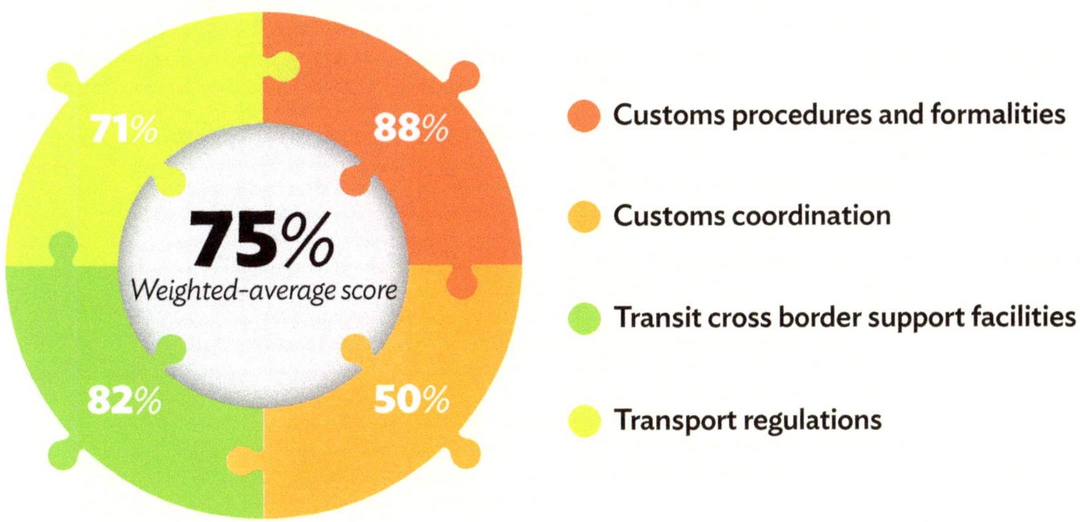

Source: Study team's calculations based on the Cross-Border Trade and Transport Facilitation Index survey.

Customs procedures and formalities

In this area, the BCP scored 71%, due to the digitalization of customs processing across the border (Figure 36). There is provision to process the requisite documents electronically by customs including passport, commercial driver's license, permit for vehicle entry, insurance certificates, customs bond, cargo manifest, SPS certificate, among other documents. There is also necessary ICT infrastructure such as automated customs management system, digital payment of customs duties and taxes, electronic queue management systems with application for customs refunds, nonintrusive cargo inspection equipment, and many more sophisticated systems in place at the BCP.

Prior intimation of inspection requirements upon risk assessment, testing and/or certification requirements, and pre-arrival clearance are also provided based on the submission of information for customs clearance. However, customs officials have overriding and/or discretionary powers to carry out physical inspections beyond the findings and recommendations of risk management systems, which accounts for 5%–10% of physical inspection.

Because data for inbound traffic are not available, the outbound CPMM TFIs (2023) have been considered for Torkham and then compared with the inbound data of the other BCPs selected under the analysis. The time taken to cross the border is on the higher side, at 30 hours for outbound traffic, while the cost incurred to cross is around $270. As a result, this BCP scored 0 on both TFIs (Figure 36).

Figure 36: Performance of Torkham Border Crossing Point on Customs Procedures and Formalities

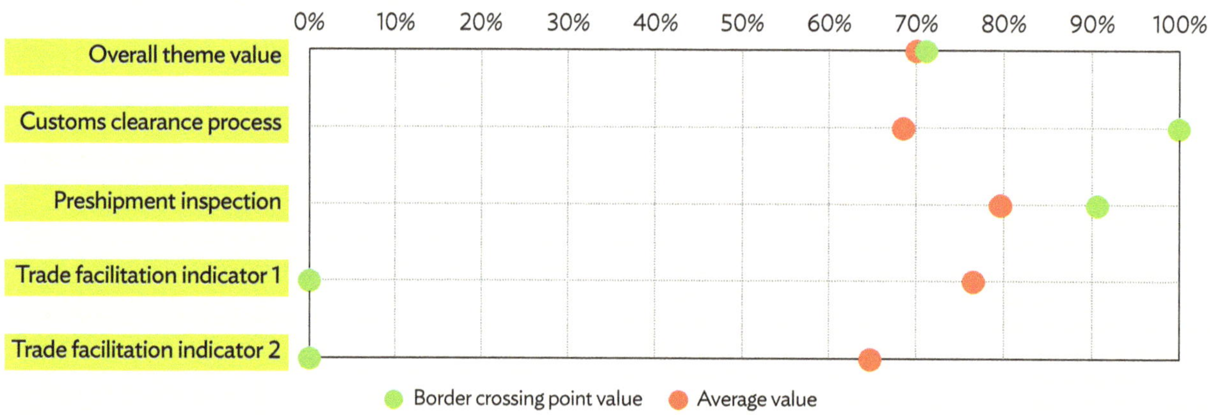

Note: "Average value" here refers to the average score for each parameter across the six shortlisted border crossing points.
Source: Study team's calculations based on the Cross-Border Trade and Transport Facilitation Index survey.

Customs coordination

Torkham BCP has secured the highest score, 88%, on the customs coordination theme, due to its synchronization mechanism with the neighboring BCP (Figure 37). Customs authorities report having provisions of joint customs control operations such as synchronized clearance procedures, electronic data exchange and interoperable information systems between customs authorities to expedite the clearance process. However, the actual extent of on-ground implementation of the same remains to be ascertained. Mutual recognition of documents like authorized economic operator certification, vehicle registration permits, driver's license and SPS certificates, among others, are enabled for the BCP.

Since the border crossing operates only 9 hours during daytime, it scores only 25% on *operating hours %*, below the average value of 75% of other BCPs (Figure 37).

Figure 37: Performance of Torkham Border Crossing Point on Customs Coordination

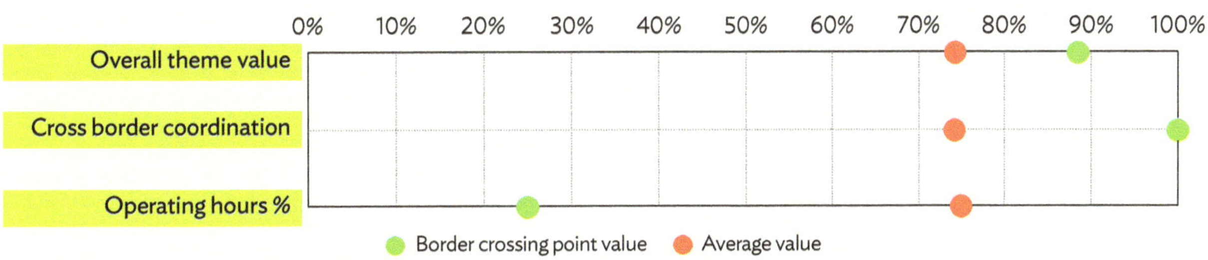

Note: "Average value" here refers to the average score for each parameter across the six shortlisted border crossing points.
Source: Study team's calculations based on the Cross-Border Trade and Transport Facilitation Index survey.

Transit cross-border support facilities

In this theme, the BCP has also secured the highest overall score of 82% (Figure 38). Major logistic infrastructure such as logistics hub, dry ports, general storage and/or customs bonded warehouses, cargo transloading terminals, material handling equipment for heavy cargo and electric power generators are available at the BCP, facilitating faster clearances.

The utilization ratio for the BCP is currently 0.65, and expected to increase given expected annual traffic growth at 20%. The time efficiency index for the border crossing comes out as 14.3 trucks per lane per hour, indicating not much delay in processing of customs cargo trucks. Accordingly, the border crossing scored 50% and 68% on the *utilization ratio* and *time efficiency ratio* indicator (Figure 38).

Figure 38: Performance of Torkham Border Crossing Point on Transit Cross-Border Support Facilities

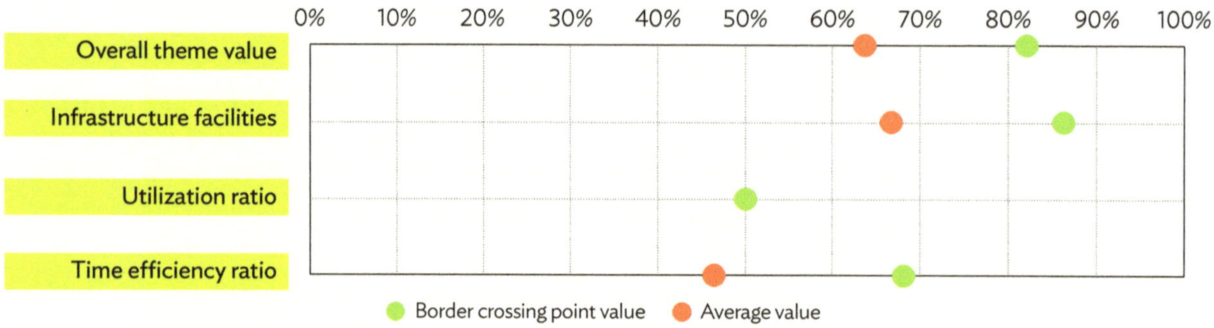

Note: "Average value" here refers to the average score for each parameter across the six shortlisted border crossing points.
Source: Study team's calculations based on the Cross-Border Trade and Transport Facilitation Index survey.

Transport regulations

The BCP scores 50% for the transport regulations, since there are weight limitations for cargo vehicles to cross. However, there are no dimension limitations for truck and container vehicles. At the Torkham border crossing between Pakistan and Afghanistan, vehicle weight regulations are enforced to maintain road safety and infrastructure integrity. The Afghanistan–Pakistan Transit Trade Agreement limits various truck configurations: for example: 6-wheeler trucks (2-axle single): up to 12 tons, 10-wheeler trucks (3-axle tandem): up to 22 tons, and 12-wheeler trucks (4-axle tridem): up to 31 tons.[14]

Table 10 presents the key findings from the CBTTFI on the likely factors contributing to higher costs or delays across CPMM activities at the Torkham border crossing.

Table 10: Torkham—Analysis of Corridor Performance Measurement and Monitoring Activities Based on Cross-Border Trade and Transport Facilitation Index Findings

S. No.	CPMM Activity	CPMM Value		Findings from CBTTFI Survey Attributing to Higher CPMM Value
		Time	Cost	
1	**Border security and/or control**	IN: – OUT: –	IN: – OUT: –	• Officials have overriding and/or discretionary powers to carry out physical inspections beyond findings of computerized risk assessment algorithms which account for 5%–10% inspection, which may lead to higher time taken to cross the BCP. • However, given that the customs authorities have reported very high BCP cargo handling capacity with 12 exclusive lanes for truck cargo examination, along with the availability of most of the key ICT systems for faster processing, there seems to be a disconnect between the CPMM TFI 1 value reported for this activity with the inputs received on CBTTFI for this BCP.
2	**Customs controls**	IN: – OUT: **24.8 hrs**	IN: – OUT: **$237**	

continued on next page

[14] Afghanistan–Pakistan Transit Trade Agreement (Kabul, Afghanistan, 2010), Article 12, p.37.

Table 10 *continued*

S. No.	CPMM Activity	CPMM Value: Time	CPMM Value: Cost	Findings from CBTTFI Survey Attributing to Higher CPMM Value
3	**Commercial inspection**	IN: – OUT: –	IN: – OUT: –	• No gaps identified under the CBTTFI survey
4	**Health and/or quarantine**	IN: – OUT: –	IN: – OUT: –	
5	**Phytosanitary**	IN: – OUT: –	IN: – OUT: –	
6	**Veterinary inspection**	IN: – OUT: –	IN: – OUT: –	
7	**Visa and/or immigration**	IN: – OUT: **1.7 hrs**	IN: – OUT: **$0**	• Mandatory physical submission of passport/national ID card
8	**Transit conformity**	IN: – OUT: –	IN: – OUT: –	• No gaps identified under the CBTTFI survey
9	**GAI and/or traffic inspection**	IN: – OUT: –	IN: – OUT: –	• No gaps identified under the CBTTFI survey
10	**Police checkpoint or stop**	IN: – OUT: –	IN: – OUT: –	• Mandatory physical submission for commercial driver's license
11	**Transport inspection**	IN: – OUT: –	IN: – OUT: –	
12	**Weight and/or standard inspection**	IN: – OUT: **0.7 hrs**	IN: – OUT: **$10**	• No gaps identified under the CBTTFI survey
13	**Vehicle registration**	IN: – OUT: –	IN: – OUT: –	• Mandatory physical submission for vehicle registration document and permit for vehicle entry
14	**Emergency repair**	IN: – OUT: –	IN: – OUT: –	• No gaps identified under the CBTTFI survey
15	**Escort or convoy**	IN: – OUT: –	IN: – OUT: –	• No gaps identified under the CBTTFI survey
16	**Loading and unloading**	IN: – OUT: **4.3 hrs**	IN: – OUT: **$50**	• No gaps identified under the CBTTFI survey • However, given that the customs authorities have reported to have most of the requisite infrastructure in place at the BCP itself, there seems to be a disconnect between the CPMM TFI 1 value reported for this activity with the inputs received on CBTTFI for this BCP.
17	**Road or bridge toll**	IN: – OUT: –	IN: – OUT: –	• No gaps identified under the CBTTFI survey
18	**Waiting or queueing**	IN: – OUT: **4.7 hrs**	IN: – OUT: –	• The BCP is operational for only 8 to 9 hours a day, which may impact the cargo traffic at the BCP. However, given that the customs authorities have reported very high BCP cargo handling capacity with 12 exclusive lanes for truck cargo examination, along with the availability of most of the key ICT systems for faster processing, there seems to be a disconnect between the CPMM TFI 1 value reported for 'Waiting or queueing' activity with the inputs received on CBTTFI for this BCP.

BCP = border crossing point, CBTTFI = Cross-Border Trade and Transport Facilitation Index, CPMM = corridor performance measurement and monitoring, GAI = Gosudarstvennaya Avtomobilnaya Inspektsiya (State Automobile Inspectorate in Russian), ICT = information and communication technology, IN = inbound traffic, OUT = outbound traffic, TFI = trade facilitation indicator.

Source: Study team's findings based on Cross-Border Trade and Transport Facilitation Index analysis.

Case Study 6: Yallama, Uzbekistan

Yallama BCP is located in the Tashkent region of Uzbekistan on CAREC corridors 3 and 6, acting as a customs and logistics terminal near the border with Kazakhstan. This BCP is Uzbekistan's second busiest, connecting the country to Russian and European markets, and facilitating transit through Kazakhstan and the PRC to and from South Asia and East Asia (ADB n.d).

The border crossing has five lanes for truck examination with maximum cargo handling capacity of 30,000 trucks and/or containers per month (footnote 10). Annual traffic is expected to be 20%–25% for the next 5 years (footnote 10).

The top-three cargo commodities crossing are consumer goods (fast-moving consumer goods), knitwear and timber, with the peak months for border passage are March, May, June, and September to December. The border crossing is operational 24 hours daily in coordination with Konysbayeva BCP in Kazakhstan.

Yallama border crossing scored a total weighted average of 77% across the various themes of the CBTTFI, with a snapshot in Figure 39.

Figure 39: Performance of Yallama Border Crossing Point

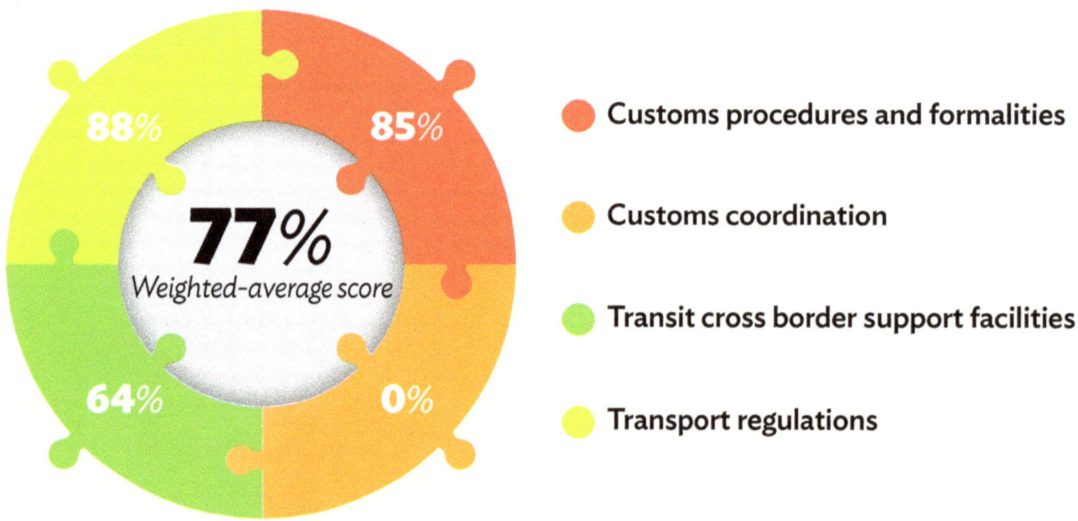

Source: Study team's calculations based on the Cross-Border Trade and Transport Facilitation Index survey.

Customs procedures and formalities

The BCP has performed well, scoring 88% on the customs procedures and formalities theme (Figure 40). There is a provision to process documents electronically by customs for most requisite documents, including passport, commercial driver's license, vehicle registration permit, insurance certificate, customs bond, cargo manifest, and customs declaration among other documents. Customs ICT infrastructure like automated management system, digital payment of duties, nonintrusive cargo inspection equipment, and computerized transit control systems are also present. Prior intimation of testing and/or certification requirements with provision to make advance fee payment for inspections are provided at the BCP.

Although inspections take place based on computerized risk-based assessment, the customs authorities have overriding and/or discretionary powers to carry out physical inspections beyond the findings. In total, 5%–10% of physical inspections are carried out in a year.

The CPMM TFIs (2023), time taken to cross the BCP comes out as only 1.1 hours for inbound traffic indicating faster processing (leading to a score of 99%), while the cost incurred to cross the BCP is only $15 which is the least cost among the selected BCPs (leading to 100% score) (Figure 40).

Figure 40: Performance of Yallama Border Crossing Point on Customs Procedures and Formalities

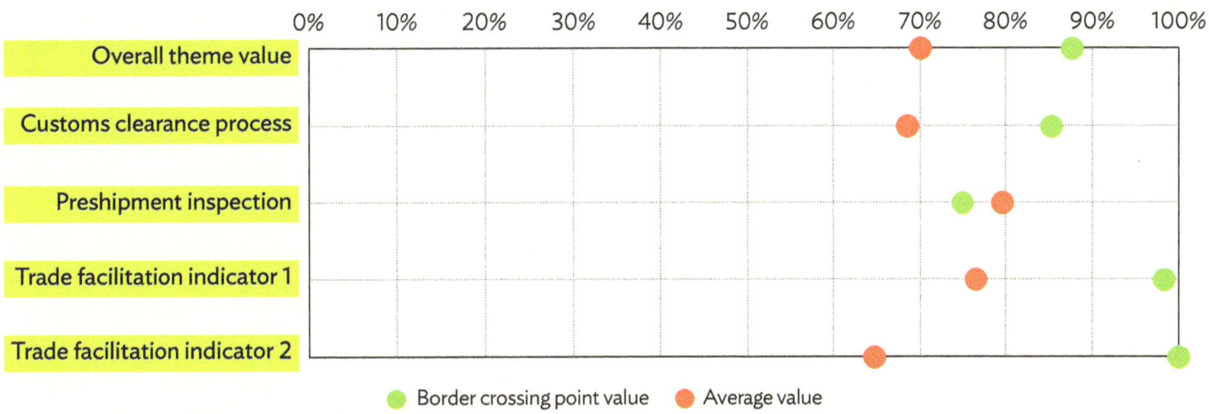

Note: "Average value" here refers to the average score for each parameter across the six shortlisted border crossing points.
Source: Study team's calculations based on the Cross-Border Trade and Transport Facilitation Index survey.

Customs coordination

The BCP has also shown good performance and scored 85% on the customs coordination front (Figure 41). Customs authorities report having provisions of interoperable information systems between customs authorities at the BCP. However, the actual extent of cross-border interoperability and on-ground implementation of the same remains to be ascertained.

Mutual recognition of requisite documents including authorized economic operator certification, driver's license, vehicle registration permits, SPS certificates, and insurance documents among others are also provisioned in the BCP. However, synchronized clearance procedures between customs authorities could be implemented at the BCP to enhance the customs processing.

The BCP operates 24 hours a day (operational hours: 100%) in synchronization with neighboring Konysbayeva BCP in Kazakhstan to process around 30,000 maximum cargo trucks in a month (Figure 41).

Figure 41: Performance of Yallama Border Crossing Point on Customs Coordination

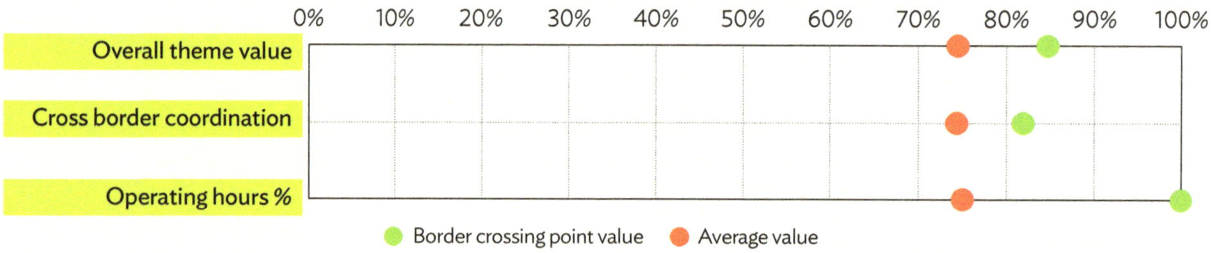

Note: "Average value" here refers to the average score for each parameter across the six shortlisted border crossing points.
Source: Study team's calculations based on the Cross-Border Trade and Transport Facilitation Index survey.

Transit cross-border support facilities

While logistics hub, customs bonded warehouse, cargo transloading terminals, and electric power generators are available at the BCP, many logistic infrastructure facilities like general storage and/or cold storage warehouses, fueling stations, and industrial parks and/or clusters are present only in the vicinity of the BCP. The BCP scored 64% under the transit cross-border support facilities theme, which is the same as the overall average score of 64% (Figure 42).

The utilization ratio for the BCP is 0.89, indicating high operational efficiency, securing 100% on this indicator. On the other hand, the time efficiency index for the border point comes out as 7.4 trucks per lane per hour, scoring 26%, lower than the average score of 46%, indicating scope for improvement (Figure 42).

Figure 42: Performance of Yallama Border Crossing Point on Transit Cross-Border Support Facilities

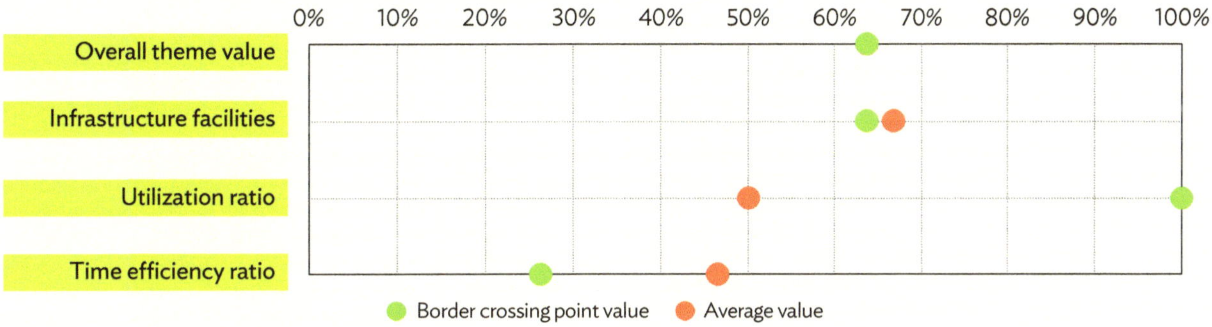

Note: "Average value" here refers to the average score for each parameter across the six shortlisted border crossing points.
Source: Study team's calculations based on the Cross-Border Trade and Transport Facilitation Index survey.

Transport regulations

Given transport regulations, weight and dimension limitations exist for cargo vehicles. The permissible maximum height is 4 meters, width of 2.55 meters, and the maximum length of 12 meters for a truck or trailer, with an articulated vehicle's maximum length up to 20 meters (UNESCAP n.d). The weight limit per single axle reaches 10 tons of cargo (UNESCAP n.d). These restrictions are mainly placed to regulate the traffic through the BCP, which contains both passenger and freight vehicles. Due to these limitations, the BCP has not attained the desired score.

Table 11 presents the key findings from the CBTTFI on the likely factors contributing to higher costs or delays across CPMM activities at the Yallama BCP.

Table 11: Yallama—Analysis of Corridor Performance Measurement and Monitoring Activities Based on Cross-Border Trade and Transport Facilitation Index Findings

S. No.	CPMM Activity	CPMM Value		Findings from CBTTFI Survey Attributing to Higher CPMM Value
		Time	Cost	
1	**Border security and/or control**	IN: **0.2 hrs** OUT: **0.1 hrs**	IN: **$5** OUT: **-**	• Officials have overriding and/or discretionary powers to carry out physical inspections beyond findings of computerized risk assessment algorithms which account for 5%–10% inspection • Synchronized clearance procedures and electronic data interchange between customs authorities are not present currently
2	**Customs controls**	IN: **0.4 hrs** OUT: **0.2 hrs**	IN: **$35** OUT: **-**	

continued on next page

Table 11 *continued*

S. No.	CPMM Activity	CPMM Value		Findings from CBTTFI Survey Attributing to Higher CPMM Value
		Time	Cost	
3	Commercial inspection	IN: –	IN: –	• Even though border control staff are available at all times for undertaking inspections, delays still happen from time to time; more staff could be deployed
		OUT: –	OUT: –	
4	Health and/or quarantine	IN: 0.1 hrs	IN: $5	
		OUT: 0.1 hrs	OUT: $5	
5	Phytosanitary	IN: 0.1 hrs	IN: $5	
		OUT: 0.1 hrs	OUT: $5	
6	Veterinary inspection	IN: 0.1 hrs	IN: –	
		OUT: –	OUT: –	
7	Visa and/or immigration	IN: 0.1 hrs	IN: –	• Mandatory physical submission of passport/national ID card
		OUT: 0.1 hrs	OUT: $5	
8	Transit conformity	IN: 0.2 hrs	IN: $13	• No gaps identified under the CBTTFI survey
		OUT: 0.1 hrs	OUT: –	
9	GAI and/or traffic inspection	IN: –	IN: –	• No gaps identified under the CBTTFI survey
		OUT: –	OUT: –	
10	Police checkpoint or stop	IN: –	IN: –	• Mandatory physical submission for commercial driver's license
		OUT: –	OUT: –	
11	Transport inspection	IN: –	IN: –	
		OUT: 0.1 hrs	OUT: –	
12	Weight and/or standard inspection	IN: 0.1 hrs	IN: –	• No gaps identified under the CBTTFI survey
		OUT: 0.1 hrs	OUT: –	
13	Vehicle registration	IN: –	IN: –	• Mandatory physical submission for vehicle registration document and permit for vehicle entry
		OUT: 0.2 hrs	OUT: –	
14	Emergency repair	IN: –	IN: –	• No gaps identified under the CBTTFI survey
		OUT: –	OUT: –	
15	Escort or convoy	IN: –	IN: –	• No gaps identified under the CBTTFI survey
		OUT: –	OUT: –	
16	Loading and unloading	IN: –	IN: –	• No gaps identified under the CBTTFI survey
		OUT: –	OUT: –	
17	Road or bridge toll	IN: –	IN: –	• No gaps identified under the CBTTFI survey
		OUT: –	OUT: –	
18	Waiting or queueing	IN: 2.0 hrs	IN: $0	• The time efficiency index for the BCP comes out as 7.4 trucks per lane per hour, scoring 26%, which is lower than the average score of 46% indicating scope for improvement
		OUT: 3.4 hrs	OUT: –	

BCP = border crossing point, CBTTFI = Cross-Border Trade and Transport Facilitation Index, CPMM = corridor performance measurement and monitoring, GAI = Gosudarstvennaya Avtomobilnaya Inspektsiya (State Automobile Inspectorate in Russian) IN = inbound traffic, OUT = outbound traffic.

Source: Study team's findings based on the Cross-Border Trade and Transport Facilitation Index analysis.

5 Key Recommendations for Selected Border Crossing Points

Recommendations for Improving Selected Border Crossing Points

The Cross-Border Trade and Transport Facilitation Index (CBTTFI) framework has helped analyze the selected BCPs in the CAREC region across the themes of customs procedures, customs coordination, transit cross-border support facilities, and transport regulations. This exercise has aimed to identify gaps or limitations in these BCPs, assess their performance relative to other border crossings within the same country (intra-country performance), and compare them with BCPs in other CAREC countries (inter-country performance), complementing the CPMM data findings for these border crossings. Ultimately, the exercise aims to foster healthy competition within the CAREC region to enhance trade and transport facilitation.

Figure 43 provides a snapshot of the scores for each BCP analyzed along with the mean score.[15]

At the theme level, Yallama BCP of Uzbekistan scored highest in customs procedures and formalities (88%), while Torkham BCP of Pakistan scored highest in customs coordination (88%) and support facilities (82%), and Turkmenistan's Serhetabat and Farap BCPs secured top scores on the transport regulations theme (100%). The score by theme of each BCP is given in Figure 44.

However, when theme weightages are adjusted within the proposed range outlined in the methodology, the weighted average scores for the BCPs vary by 1%–3% based on the given set of survey responses.

[15] While CPMM data indicates that BCPs like Tsiteli Khidi in Georgia have shorter crossing times—suggesting faster clearance, the CBTTFI survey places greater emphasis on digitalization within the customs procedures and formalities theme and the support infrastructure and customs coordination theme. Within these focus areas, Torkham has performed strongly, contributing to its higher overall weighted average score among the selected border points. Notably, a state-of-the-art Integrated Transit Trade Management System is being developed at Torkham, featuring dedicated import and export yards with parking capacity for 400 trucks and 100 light vehicles. Modern administrative facilities and a dedicated business hub—housing banks, internet services, and clearing agents—have been established at the terminal. Advanced equipment such as gantry scanners, pass-through scanners, under-vehicle scanners, weighing scales, and explosives/narcotics detection devices have also been installed. Comprehensive security is further supported through biometric data collection, luggage scanning systems, and an RFID-based passenger management system using e-gates and e-passports. Torkham also benefits from the integration of the WeBOC platform with Pakistan's Single Window Portal, enabling real-time data sharing across ministries and departments. Moreover, electronic data interchange with regional trading partners and digital end-to-end container tracking through geo-fencing enhance the transparency and efficiency of cross-border trade operations. See https://www.thenews.com.pk/print/1263118-ittms-at-torkham-chaman-90pc-complete; https://tribune.com.pk/story/2516773/97-work-on-modern-border-terminals-at-torkham-chaman-completed; and CAREC – Regional Improving Borders (RIBS) Project. https://www.carecprogram.org/uploads/RIBS-Pakistan-Module-1.pdf (all accessed 7 May 2025).

Figure 43: Scores for Border Crossing Point Under the Cross-Border Trade and Transport Facilitation Index

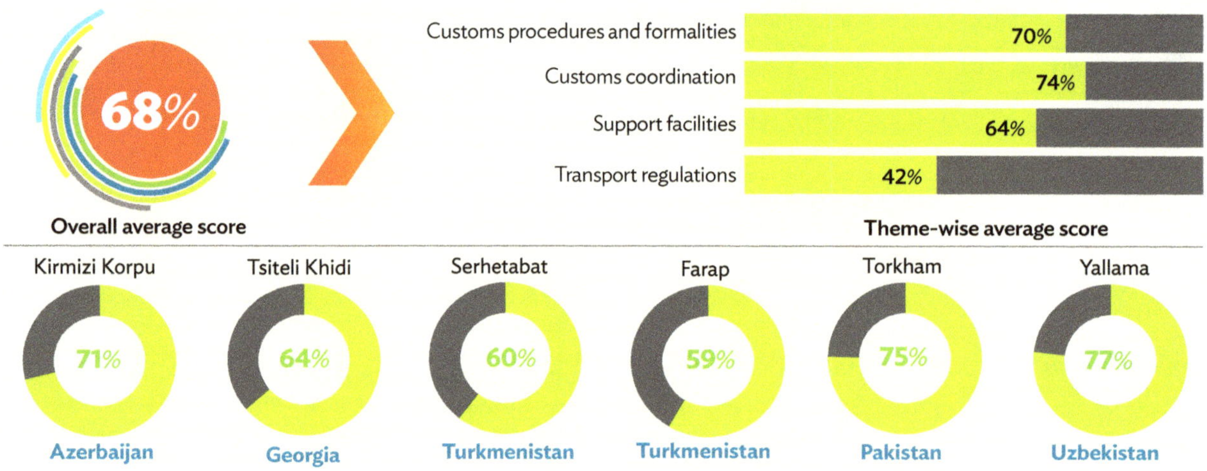

Source: Study team's calculations based on the Cross-Border Trade and Transport Facilitation Index survey.

Figure 44: Scores for Border Crossing Points Under the Cross-Border Trade and Transport Facilitation Index, by Theme

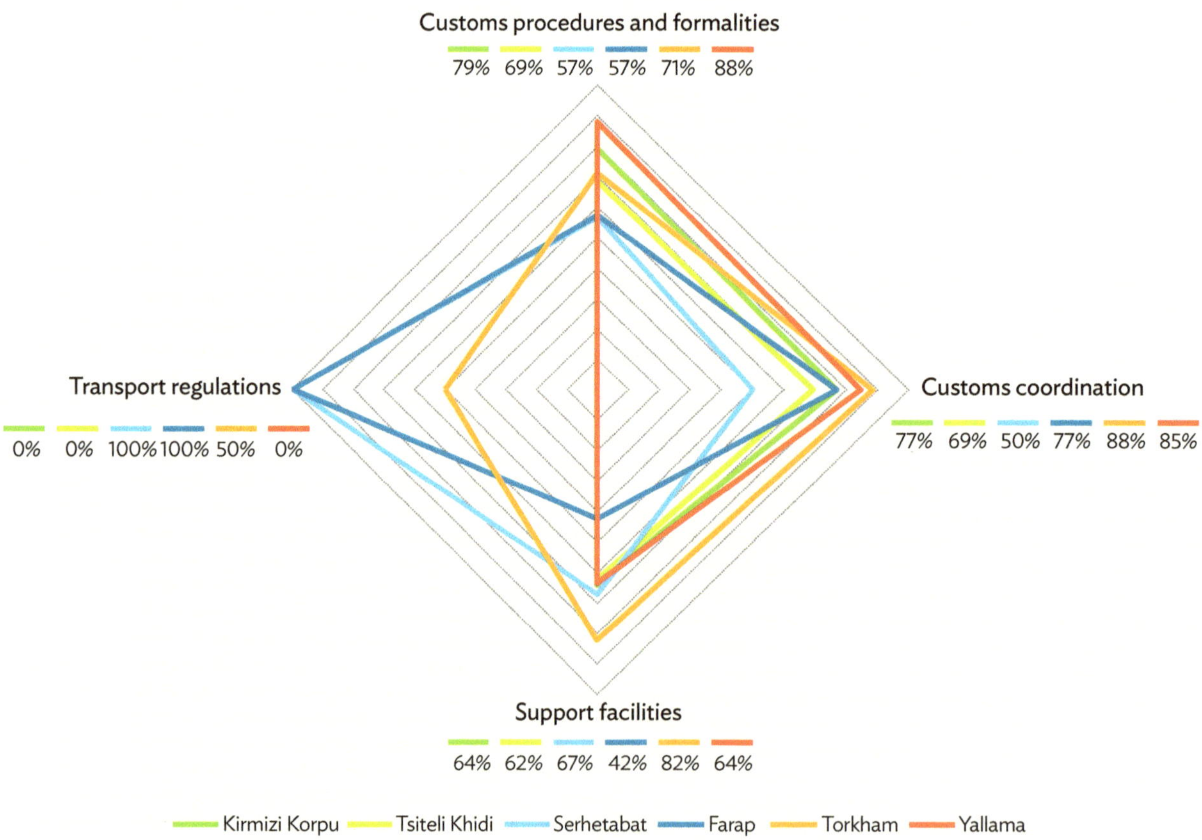

Source: Study team's calculations based on the Cross-Border Trade and Transport Facilitation Index survey.

Below are some of the key recommendations for the BCPs, categorized into five broad themes.

5.1.1 Enhance Customs Efficiency and Transparency

Customs procedures are often a significant part of cross-border trade. Streamlining these processes reduces delays, lowers transaction costs, and increases the overall volume of trade. For CAREC member countries, many of which are landlocked, efficient customs procedures can make trade easier and more cost-effective, thus fostering economic growth and integration. Transparency in customs operations reduces the opportunity for bribery and corruption, which are common challenges in border management. By standardizing and simplifying customs procedures, countries can better integrate with each other and also with other international trade partners. This fosters stronger economic relationships and promotes regional stability and collaboration. The suggested recommendations in line with promoting customs efficiency and transparency are detailed further.

Recommendation 1: Digitalization of customs processes at the border crossing points

Digitalization refers to the adoption of modern technology and digital tools to streamline and automate procedures involved in cross-border trade. Rather than relying solely on the physical submission of paper forms, businesses and customs officials can use electronic data processing systems to submit and exchange trade-related documents, such as customs declarations, invoices, certificates of origin, bills of lading, vehicle registration permits, and cargo manifest, among others (ADB 2022a). This significantly reduces paperwork, minimizes errors, and speeds up the clearance process. Through digital platforms, businesses can submit the necessary documentation and receive approval for customs clearance before arriving at the border. This enables customs authorities to pre-clear shipments, which can expedite the process upon arrival at the border.

Importantly, such digital systems are not intended to replace the requirement for original documents where mandated by law—such as passports, visas, driver's licenses, or certain shipping documents—but rather to complement them by enabling faster verification and risk-based targeting. Digitalization also allows customs authorities to apply risk management tools, such as data analytics and machine learning, to assess the risk of shipments before they arrive. Low-risk shipments can be processed quickly, while higher-risk shipments can be flagged for further inspection. This ensures efficient resource use. Still, physical copies of original documents should be present for customs verification to maintain safety and security at the border-crossing.

Figure 45 provides levels of electronic customs processing implementation for key documents in the analyzed BCPs.

Figure 45: Performance of Border Crossing Points Under Digitalization of Customs Processes

	Kirmizi Korpu Azerbaijan	Tsiteli Khidi Georgia	Serhetabat Turkmenistan	Farap Turkmenistan	Torkham Pakistan	Yallama Uzbekistan
Passport/national ID	◔	◔	◔	●	●	●
Visa	◑	◔	◔	◔	○	○
Commercial driver's license	◔	◔	◔	◔	●	●
Permit for vehicle entry	●	◔	◔	◔	●	●
Vehicle registration document	◔	◔	◔	◔	●	●
Certificate of liability insurance	◔	◔	○	○	●	●
Certificate of cargo insurance	○	○	○	○	●	●
Official weight ticket	●	○	○	○	●	○
TIR carnet/customs bond	◔	◔	●	◑	●	●
Bill of lading	○	○	○	○	●	○
CMR consignment note	●	◔	◔	◔	●	●
Packaging list/cargo manifest	●	○	◔	◔	●	●
Customs declaration	●	◑	●	◔	●	◔
Certificate of origin	●	○	○	○	●	●
SPS certificate	●	◔	○	○	●	○
Commercial inspection certificate	○	○	○	○	●	○
Standard conformance certificate	○	○	○	○	●	●
Commercial invoice	●	◔	◔	◔	●	●

● Provision to process documents electronically by customs ◑ Provision to upload documents in electronic system prior to arrival ◔ Mandatory physical submission of original document ○ Not applicable/ No response

CMR = Convention on the Contract for the International Carriage of Goods by Road, SPS = sanitary and phytosanitary, TIR = Transports Internationaux Routiers (International Road Transport).

Source: Study team's analysis based on the Cross-Border Trade and Transport Facilitation Index survey responses.

Based on the analysis, systems are needed that allow cargo carriers to electronically upload key documents in advance (Table 12). While original physical copies may still be required for final verification where mandated, the ability to pre-submit electronic copies of supporting documents can significantly reduce delays, improve queue management, and enhance overall processing efficiency.

Table 12: Border Crossing Point Recommendations for Electronic Processing of Documents

#	BCP	Documents Requiring Provisions for Electronic Upload and Processing
1	**Kirmizi Korpu, Azerbaijan**	Passport and/or national ID, commercial driver's license, vehicle registration document, certificate of liability insurance, TIR carnet/customs bond
2	**Tsiteli Khidi, Georgia**	Passport and/or national ID, visa, commercial driver's license, permit for vehicle entry, vehicle registration document, certificate of liability insurance, TIR carnet/customs bond, CMR consignment note, SP certificate, commercial invoice
3	**Serhetabat, Turkmenistan**	Passport and/or national ID, visa, commercial driver's license, permit for vehicle entry, vehicle registration document, TIR carnet/customs bond, CMR consignment note, packaging list/cargo manifest, commercial invoice
4	**Farap, Turkmenistan**	Visa, commercial driver's license, permit for vehicle entry, vehicle registration document, CMR consignment note, packaging list/cargo manifest, customs declaration, commercial invoice
5	**Yallama, Uzbekistan**	Customs declaration

CMR = Convention on the Contract for the International Carriage of Goods by Road, ID = identity, SPS = sanitary and phytosanitary, TIR = Transports Internationaux Routiers (International Road Transport).

Source: Study team's suggestions based on the Cross-Border Trade and Transport Facilitation Index analysis.

Recommendation 2: Inclusion of ICT infrastructure at the border crossing points

The integration of robust ICT infrastructure at a BCP enhances efficiency, transparency, and security by streamlining processes, minimizing manual intervention, and ensuring real-time monitoring. Automated systems such as single window portals, customs management platforms, and electronic payment solutions accelerate documentation and customs clearance, reducing delays and improving operational efficiency (ADB 2022a).

Digital mechanisms for customs refunds, queue management, and SPS inspections enhance transparency, enabling stakeholders to track shipments and declarations seamlessly. Further, security is reinforced through nonintrusive cargo inspection, automated passport control, video surveillance, and radiation detection, mitigating risks while facilitating smooth cross-border movement.

Automated systems also improve data accuracy, reduce human errors, and support effective decision-making, strengthening compliance and risk management.

The degree of ICT infrastructure implementation in the analyzed border crossing is given in Figure 46.

Figure 46: Performance of Border Crossing Points Under Inclusion of Information and Communication Technology Infrastructure

	Kirmizi Korpu Azerbaijan	Tsiteli Khidi Georgia	Serhetabat Turkmenistan	Farap Turkmenistan	Torkham Pakistan	Yallama Uzbekistan
Single window portal	●	●	●	●	●	●
Automated customs management system	●	●	●	●	●	●
Digital payment of duties/taxes	●	●	○	○	●	●
Electronic application for customs refunds	○	○	○	○	●	●
Electronic queue management system	●	●	○	○	●	●
Nonintrusive cargo inspection equipment	●	●	●	●	●	●
Computerized transit control systems	●	●	●	●	●	●
Automated passport control systems	●	●	●	○	●	●
Video surveillance systems	●	●	●	●	●	●
Automatic radiation detection systems	●	●	●	●	●	●
Portable illegal drug identification systems	●	●	●	●	●	●
Automated system for SPS inspection and declarations	●	●	●	●	●	●
e-TIR	●	●	○	○	●	●
e-CMR	○	○	○	○	●	●
Customs mobile app	●	○	●	●	●	●

● Presence of infrastructure ○ Absence of infrastructure

e-CMR = electronic consignment note, e-TIR = electronic Transports Internationaux Routiers, SPS = sanitary and phytosanitary.
Source: Study team's analysis based on the Cross-Border Trade and Transport Facilitation Index survey responses.

Based on this analysis, the BCPs are equipped with most requisite ICT infrastructure. Table 13 presents recommendations.

Table 13: Recommendations for Enhancing Information and Communication Technology Infrastructure Border Crossing Points

#	BCP	Recommendation
1	**Kirmizi Korpu, Azerbaijan**	• Provisioning of electronic application for customs refunds to file and track refund requests digitally, reducing paperwork, processing time, and the risk of errors or discrepancies. • Provisioning of e-CMR to facilitate digital handling of transport documents, improving cross-border logistics by enabling real-time tracking, reducing document loss, and minimizing delays. • While this BCP has most of the ICT infrastructure, the authorities may focus on improving the service level up time, specifically for Single Window portal, computerized transit control systems and portable illegal drug identification system at the BCP.
2	**Tsiteli Khidi, Georgia**	• On similar lines to Kirmizi Korpu BCP, provisioning of electronic application for customs refunds and e-CMR facility at the BCP. • Further, development of a Customs Mobile Application to improve user experience, streamline operations, and enhance overall trade facilitation by making customs-related services more accessible, reducing paperwork, and enabling faster decision-making.
3	**Serhetabat, Turkmenistan**	• Introducing the following ICT provisions: • Digital payment of duties/taxes to ensure faster, more secure, and transparent transactions, reducing the risk of errors or fraud. • Electronic application for customs refunds to speed up approvals and enhance accountability. • Electronic Queue Management System to optimize resource allocation, reduce wait times, and improve the overall flow of traffic. • e-TIR (Electronic Transit System) to facilitate secure, real-time data exchange between customs administrations, expediting transit movements and reducing costs. • e-CMR (Electronic Consignment Note) to enable real-time data sharing, ensuring smoother cross-border logistics and better integration with international trade systems.
4	**Farap, Turkmenistan**	• On similar lines to Serhetabat BCP, introducing digital payment of duties/taxes, electronic application for customs refunds, electronic queue management system, E-TIR, e-CMR as well as automated passport control systems to accelerate identity verification and enhance security checks.
5	**Torkham, Pakistan**	• While the Torkham BCP has all the requisite ICT infrastructure in place, their service up time needs to be improved to enhance service efficiency.

BCP = border crossing point, e-CMR = electronic consignment note, e-TIR = electronic Transports Internationaux Routiers, ICT = information and communication technology.

Source: Study team's suggestions based on the Cross-Border Trade and Transport Facilitation Index analysis.

In this context, it would be imperative to strengthen the digital literacy and skills of government officials. Countries may also need to explore innovative financing mechanisms and public–private partnerships to support digital connectivity projects at these BCPs (UNESCAP 2024a).

Box 4 showcases practices in digitalization and ICT infrastructure in various countries.

Box 4: Digitalization and Information and Communication Technology Infrastructure Development Practices by Country

Southeast Asia: Singapore

- The Woodlands Checkpoint has implemented automated systems for customs clearance, passenger processing, and vehicle inspection. This includes the use of electronic customs declarations (e-customs), automated vehicle clearance systems, and advanced scanning technologies to detect contraband or potential security risks.

Central Asia: Tajikistan

- As of 2022, border-crossing time dropped from 4.7 hours to 4.1 hours and cost declined, mainly at the Dusti and Panji Poyon border crossing points. The country operates an online trade portal (https://tajtrade.tj) that provides information on importing, exporting, and transiting. It has launched a single window system that connects 11 agencies and covers 24 permits and documents (www.swcustoms.tj), as well as a system of national authorized economic operators.

East Asia: Mongolia

- Mongolia has made significant strides in modernizing its customs operations through the development of the Customs Automated Information System (CAIS) and the Customs External Portal System. These digital platforms have greatly enhanced the efficiency and transparency of customs procedures. Through CAIS, citizens and enterprises can electronically submit all types of customs declarations, make online payments, update cargo manifests, and complete automated vehicle registrations, among other key functions. The integration of these systems not only reduces processing time and administrative burden but also supports improved compliance and trade facilitation.

African countries

- Automatic vehicle and container recognition systems are gaining traction across the African continent, wherein the systems capture the vehicle's license plate number and container's code to monitor the goods being transported. Subsequently, this technology transmits this information to the border control officials. It enables them to compare, in a timely fashion, their database on any potential infringements previously committed by the carrier in that country. Once the feedback is received, a comprehensive risk assessment for that vehicle and goods being transported is executed to determine the appropriate law enforcement measures. These new technologies are being implemented in addition to the traditional video surveillance systems.

- Countries such as Ethiopia, Kenya, South Africa, Sudan, and Tunisia, among others, have adopted drone technology to enhance their monitoring surveillance systems against smuggling illegal firearms and drugs. Such drone technologies coupled with smart digital technological systems can send warning messages to border control officers and encourage information sharing between law enforcement agencies.

Sources: ADB 2022c, African Union Development Agency – NEPAD. https://www.nepad.org/blog/enhancing-border-security-africa-using-smart-border-control-technologies and Montsame. https://mof.montsame.mn/en/read/333165.

The *Role of Advanced Technologies in Cross-Border Trade: A Customs Perspective* by the WTO and World Customs Organization, also shows that a number of advanced technologies have had a significant impact on customs procedures. These technologies will continue to benefit the work of customs authorities and include developments in blockchain, Internet of Things, big data analytics, artificial intelligence, and machine learning, biometrics, drones, virtual and augmented reality, and 3-D printing (WCO and WTO n.d). These developments may also be useful for CAREC countries to adopt to enhance trade facilitation, improve customs efficiency, and strengthen regional connectivity.

5.1.2 Coordinate Border-Crossing Operations

Given the region's diverse economic backgrounds, geography, and varying customs practices, effective coordination among customs authorities at BCPs is essential for facilitating smoother trade flows, reducing delays, minimizing costs, and enhancing regional integration. The recommendation for coordination of cross-border operations is detailed further.

Recommendation 3: Synchronization of customs procedures at the border crossing points

CAREC member countries can work toward harmonizing customs rules and regulations across borders. This includes implementing interoperable information systems with electronic data interchange between customs authorities, harmonized clearance procedures, and mutual recognition of submitted documents (UNECE 2012). By standardizing the customs procedures, the region reduces complexity and allows more predictable and efficient trade operations.

Coordination between customs agencies at border points allows joint inspections and harmonized procedures. This eliminates the need for multiple agencies to conduct separate inspections, reducing waiting times for traders. It also enhances the consistency of joint customs control operations across different border points in the region. Customs coordination mechanisms in the analyzed BCPs are given in Figure 47.

Figure 47: Performance of Border Crossing Points Under Customs Coordination Operations

	Kirmizi Korpu Azerbaijan	Tsiteli Khidi Georgia	Serhetabat Turkmenistan	Farap Turkmenistan	Torkham Pakistan	Yallama Uzbekistan
Interoperable information systems	●	●	●	●	●	●
Synchronized clearance procedure	●	●	●	●	●	●
Electronic data interchange	●	●	○	○	●	●
MR – inspection certificates	○	○	○	○	●	●
MR – inspection certificates	●	●	○	○	●	●
MR – AEO certification	●	●	●	●	●	●
MR – vehicle registration permits	●	●	●	●	●	●
MR – customs guarantee for transport/cargo	●	●	●	○	●	●
MR – driver's license	●	●	●	●	●	●
MR – insurance documents	●	●	●	●	●	●
MR – quality certifications	●	●	●	●	●	●

● Presence of provision ○ Absence of provision

AEO = authorized economic operator, MR = mutual recognition, SPS = sanitary and phytosanitary.
Source: Study team's analysis based on the Cross-Border Trade and Transport Facilitation Index survey responses.

Customs coordination mechanisms such as interoperable information systems, electronic data interchange between customs authorities, synchronized clearance procedures, and mutual recognition of documents are highly essential to promote transport and trade facilitation. Table 14 presents recommendations for BCPs.

Table 14: Recommendations for Harmonization of Customs Procedures at Border Crossing Points

#	Border Control Point	Recommendation
1	**Kirmizi Korpu, Azerbaijan**	• Implementing synchronized clearance procedures with neighboring BCP • Implementing mutual recognition of inspection and quality certifications, preventing redundant checks, eliminating the need for reinspections and reducing compliance costs for businesses
2	**Tsiteli Khidi, Georgia**	• Implementing interoperable information systems between customs authorities for enhancing cross-border coordination, enabling real-time data exchange, reducing redundancies, and improving trade efficiency. • Synchronizing clearance procedures with neighboring BCP • Implementing mutual recognition of AEO transporters and insurance documents

continued on next page

Table 14 *continued*

#	Border Control Point	Recommendation
3	**Serhetabat, Turkmenistan**	• Implementing interoperable information systems between customs authorities • Implementing synchronized clearance procedures with neighboring BCP • Creating provisions for mutual recognition of inspection/SPS certificates and AEO certificates
4	**Farap, Turkmenistan**	• Creating provisions for mutual recognition of inspection/SPS certificates and AEO certificates
5	**Yallama, Uzbekistan**	• Implementing synchronized clearance procedures and electronic data interchange between customs authorities

AEO = authorized economic operator, BCP = border crossing point, SPS = sanitary and phytosanitary.
Source: Study team's suggestions based on the Cross-Border Trade and Transport Facilitation Index analysis.

Notably, Kirmizi Korpu and Tsiteli Khidi BCPs share a common border. While customs authorities at both BCPs have identified the absence of synchronized clearance procedures as a challenge, only Tsiteli Khidi has highlighted the lack of interoperable information systems between customs authorities. Additionally, Kirmizi Korpu has pointed to the absence of mutual recognition for inspection and quality certifications, whereas Tsiteli Khidi has raised concerns about the lack of mutual recognition of authorized economic operator transporters and insurance documents. This discrepancy in responses underscores the need for further validation of the on-ground situation to accurately assess customs coordination challenges at both border points.

Box 5 showcases cross-border interoperability in various countries.

Box 5: Case Study of Cross Border Interoperability

Australia and New Zealand

- Whenever plant or animal products are to be exported, they often must be accompanied by appropriate certification, i.e., exchanges of electronic sanitary and phytosanitary (SPS) certificates between the Australian Quarantine and Inspection Service and New Zealand Food Safety Authority. The cross-border electronic information exchange of SPS certificates has been fully implemented and is operating efficiently between these two countries.

- Case reports of this facility have shown major benefits to the governments and business community. These include savings of about $100 per transaction and enhanced security of traded foods and agricultural products.

- Certification data directly sent and received by the government authorities of both countries reduces fraudulent activities and improves efficiency at the port of entry.

Mongolia and the People's Republic of China

- Mongolia and the People's Republic of China (PRC) have established a unified cargo manifest mechanism that first started between Erenhot (PRC) and Zamiin-Uud (Mongolia), and soon spread to other border crossing points (BCPs). Importers and exporters can declare their goods to both the PRC and Mongolian customs respectively using the same cargo manifest. There is electronic transmission of manifest data containing 18 data fields covering all information on relevant vehicles and goods, more comprehensive than the data of corresponding paper manifest.

continued on next page

Box 5 *continued*

- To enhance the customs efficiency and security of cross-border trade, the PRC and Mongolia have achieved joint customs control operations by sharing weighing data and nonintrusive inspection images of examined cargo. The customs have also implemented mutual recognition of the inspection results for particular types of container goods by sharing smart locks. One customs authority will approve the inspection results provided by the other and the shipment already inspected by neighboring customs are not examined further, to avoid redundancy.

These measures have successfully streamlined customs processes, improved accuracy in trade data, and strengthened security measures by combating false reporting and smuggling activities at border checkpoints.

Mongolia and the Russian Federation

- The customs authorities of the two countries have implemented real-time electronic exchange of export declarations. Additionally, the official exchange of truck X-ray images has commenced at the Altanbulag–Khiagt BCP. These measures enable real-time data sharing, strengthen risk management, reduce duplication of inspections, and streamline customs clearance processes. It acts as a model for successful cross-border information exchange, reducing fraud and expediting customs processes.

Sources: UNESCAP 2018, UNESCAP 2024b, ESCAP: Cross-Border Paperless Trade Database. https://www.digitalizetrade.org/projects/china-mongolia-joint-customs-control-jcc-project; ADB – Progress Report on the PRC-Mongolia Joint Customs Control. https://rksi.adb.org/wp-content/uploads/2020/09/session-3-carec-progress-report-jcc.pdf; and General Administration of Customs, PRC. http://english.customs.gov.cn/statics/fa6341a0-4999-4998-9b6e-7a8b7b473ee9.html.

5.1.3 Efficient Risk Management Operations

Efficient risk management at BCPs in the CAREC region involves several strategies aimed at ensuring the smooth flow of trade while safeguarding national security, public health, and environmental standards. These systems are designed to reduce delays, minimize the risk of illegal activities (like smuggling and human trafficking), and enhance overall trade facilitation.

The CAREC countries have adopted risk-based approaches in customs inspection, focusing on high-risk cargo based on origin, destination, and commodity type. This reduces the time spent on low-risk shipments and improves overall border efficiency. However, certain constraints found in our survey include inadequate prior intimation on inspection requirements and customs officials have discretionary powers to conduct physical inspections apart from the risk assessment which are potential factors for delays at BCPs. The recommendations suggested under efficient risk management are detailed next.

Recommendation 4: Prior intimation on testing/certification/inspection requirements before arrival at the border crossing points

Implementing a prior intimation system for testing, certification, and inspection requirements for trucks before arrival at border crossings can significantly streamline cross-border trade with the enhancement in risk management. This process requires coordination among border authorities, customs agencies, logistics operators, and businesses. The initial step is to facilitate prior intimation upon pre-arrival submission of documents with the necessary testing, certification, or inspection requirements. The platform should allow for real-time data exchange between the truck operators, customs authorities, and inspection agencies at the BCPs, ensuring all stakeholders are informed ahead of the truck's arrival. This is aided by establishing clear and standardized list of the documents and certifications required for different types of cargo, including health and safety certificates, origin certificates, phytosanitary certifications, and environmental clearance certificates (UNECE 2012). There should be set deadlines for submission of these requirements, ideally several days before the truck's scheduled arrival, to ensure timely processing and avoid congestion at the border crossings. Figure 48 summarizes the prior intimation systems in the selected BCPs.

Figure 48: Performance of Border Crossing Points Under Customs Intimation System

	Kirmizi Korpu Azerbaijan	Tsiteli Khidi Georgia	Serhetabat Turkmenistan	Farap Turkmenistan	Torkham Pakistan	Yallama Uzbekistan
Prior intimation on documentation requirements	●	●	●	●	●	●
Prior intimation on testing and/or certification requirements	●	●	○	○	●	●
Prior intimation of inspection requirement upon submission	●	○	●	●	●	●
Advance fee payment for inspections	○	●	●	●	●	●
Pre-arrival clearance based on submission of information	●	●	○	○	●	○

● Present ○ Absent

Source: Study team's analysis based on the Cross-Border Trade and Transport Facilitation Index survey responses.

Prior intimation keeps the truck drivers, traders, and transport operators well informed of the clearance requirements, which helps prevent unnecessary delays and long waiting times. Table 15 shows some of the BCP-specific recommendations.

Table 15: Recommendations for Effective Inspection Measures at Border Crossing Points

#	Border Crossing Point	Recommendation
1	**Kirmizi Korpu, Azerbaijan**	• Making provision for advance fee payment for inspections for eliminating delays caused by on-site payments, allowing seamless processing upon cargo arrival as well as reducing administrative burden on both traders and customs officials, expediting the overall clearance process.
2	**Tsiteli Khidi, Georgia**	• Implementing prior intimation of inspection requirement upon submission of pre-arrival information with customs authorities, reducing unpredictability for cargo traders, helping them plan logistics and avoid unnecessary detention.
3	**Serhetabat, Turkmenistan**	• Implementing prior intimation on testing and/or certification requirements, enabling cargo traders to arrange necessary testing and certifications before arrival, preventing delays due to missing compliance documents as well as reducing last-minute rejections or reinspections, ensuring smoother customs clearance. • Implementing the provision of pre-arrival clearance process, enabling compliant shipments to move through the border crossing point with minimal intervention, reducing dwell time at the border and enhancing trade efficiency.
4	**Farap, Turkmenistan**	
5	**Yallama, Uzbekistan**	Implementing the provision of pre-arrival clearance process at the border crossing point.

Source: Study team's suggestions based on the Cross-Border Trade and Transport Facilitation Index analysis.

Recommendation 5: Minimize overriding and/or discretionary decisions by customs officials for carrying out physical inspection beyond risk assessment

Automated risk management tools could identify high-risk consignments while minimizing physical inspection for low-risk goods as they scan shipments based on pre-set criteria and reduce subjective decision-making. Additionally, there should be clear, standard operating procedures for customs officials to follow when determining the shipments for inspection. With minimal human intervention and use of automated risk profiling, the entire customs processing could be speeded up. Figure 49 presents the automated risk decision system in the selected BCPs.

Figure 49: Performance of Border Crossing Points Under Automated Risk Decision System

	Kirmizi Korpu Azerbaijan	Tsiteli Khidi Georgia	Serhetabat Turkmenistan	Farap Turkmenistan	Torkham Pakistan	Yallama Uzbekistan
Physical inspection only based on risk assessment	●	○	●	●	○	○
Overriding/discretionary powers of officials for physical inspections	○	●	○	○	●	●

● Present ○ Absent

Source: Study team's analysis based on the Cross-Border Trade and Transport Facilitation Index survey responses.

Customs officials' overriding/discretionary powers to conduct physical inspections beyond the findings of risk assessment output could be minimized to enhance efficiency and streamline process. These steps may be taken especially in Tsiteli Khidi, Torkham, and Yallama BCPs, which would pave the way for efficient risk management.

Box 6 showcases practices adopted by various countries for risk management.

Box 6: Risk Management-Related Practices of Countries

Singapore

- Both Singapore and Malaysia have connected their customs systems to provide a seamless clearing of goods and vehicles at the Woodlands Checkpoint. This includes real-time data exchange for risk profiling, enabling customs authorities to assess potential risks more accurately and respond proactively. The checkpoint uses nonintrusive inspection technology, such as X-ray scanners, to inspect containers, trucks, and goods without having to physically open them.

- Additionally, by applying profiling methods, such as targeting high-risk consignments based on factors like the type of goods, country of origin, and trade history, authorities can prioritize inspections and focus resources on more suspicious cargo.

People's Republic of China (PRC)

- In September 2017, the PRC implemented a national trade single window, which includes its own risk-management module. This risk-management module has enabled risk-based inspections and, as a result, the overall process of export and import customs clearance has become faster.

- PRC Customs has leveraged 5G technology to develop 5G-enabled tablets and smart glasses, allowing real-time transmission of audio and video data from inspection sites to the surveillance department. This has significantly enhanced the efficiency and responsiveness of on-site supervision.

- The application of license plate recognition and facial recognition technologies enables the capture of detailed image data, breaking down data silos and creating comprehensive profiles of vehicles and individuals under supervision. This, in turn, facilitates multidimensional risk assessment, targeted inspections, and improved decision-making. Furthermore, the surveillance and command center can interact with frontline customs officers via real-time audiovisual communication, enabling direct access to inspection data. This has greatly strengthened on-site supervisory capabilities and improved coordination between field personnel and back-office departments.

Oman

- In December 2018, Oman integrated a risk-assessment system into the national Single Window, Bayan, to streamline customs clearance and physical inspections, reducing the time to comply with border requirements for imports and exports.

Source: APEC 2023 and World Bank (n.d.) AP Subnational Studies – Trading Across Borders: Good Practices. https://subnational.doingbusiness.org/en/data/exploretopics/trading-across-borders/good-practices.

5.1.4 Expand Cross-Border Transport and Logistics Infrastructure

Cross-border transit support logistics infrastructure are major requirements for faster border crossing and help enhance regional trade, economic integration, and transport connectivity. Improving and expanding the regional highway systems, particularly for the landlocked Central Asian area, with necessary logistics amenities will increase trade flows.

Recommendation 6: Inclusion of cross-border support infrastructure at the border crossing points

Establishing efficient logistics hubs at key border points would reduce congestion and enhance cargo handling capacity. Developing modern border-crossing facilities that integrate customs, security, and transport operations would facilitate smoother transitions. The BCPs could construct integrated logistics terminals at key border points, providing facilities for warehousing, cargo handling, customs processing, certification/testing, equipment for handling heavy cargo and distribution. These hubs can offer space for storage, temperature-controlled facilities, and distribution centers for goods transiting through the border.

Also, BCPs can develop dry ports at strategic locations that can act as inland customs and logistics facilities for the goods arriving via land. These dry ports can reduce congestion at actual border points by providing a buffer area where goods can be temporarily stored and processed (UNESCAP 2014). Establishing container depots at border points for the quick transfer of containerized goods between rail and truck, allowing faster processing and minimizing delays during cargo handover. The border points should take steps to set up vehicle repair and maintenance stations at border crossings for trucks and trains to address issues quickly and ensure the smooth flow of transport.

For perishable goods, establishing temperature-controlled/cold storage warehouses (considering the location and energy access for storing agricultural products) at border points can help ensure that products are stored properly while awaiting customs clearance or transfer to the next transport mode. These could be established by encouraging private sector investment through public–private partnerships, which would accelerate infrastructure development.

Figure 50 presents performance of selected BCPs under transit cross-border support facilities.

Figure 50: Performance of Border Crossing Points Under Support Logistics Infrastructure

		Kirmizi Korpu Azerbaijan	Tsiteli Khidi Georgia	Serhetabat Turkmenistan	Farap Turkmenistan	Torkham Pakistan	Yallama Uzbekistan
Hard infrastructure	Logistics hub	○	○	◑	○	●	●
	Dry ports	○	○	◑	○	●	○
	General storage warehouses	●	◑	◑	○	●	◑
	Customs bonded warehouses	●	◑	◑	◑	●	●
	Cold storage warehouses	○	○	◑	○	●	◑
	Cargo transloading terminals	●	◑	◑	●	●	●
	Secure parking lots	●	◑	◑	◑	●	●
	Maintenance repair facilities	●	◑	◑	◑	●	◑
	Vehicle fueling stations	●	◑	◑	◑	◑	◑
	Industrial parks/clusters	○	○	◑	○	◑	◑
	Free trade zones	○	○	◑	○	◑	○
	Border economic zones	○	○	◑	○	◑	○
Certification/ testing infra	Product testing labs	◑	○	◑	◑	◑	○
	Third-party inspection facilities	◑	○	◑	◑	◑	○
	Quarantine treatment centers	◑	●	◑	◑	◑	○
Equipment and system	Material handling equipment	●	○	◑	◑	●	●
	Stand-by electric generators	●	●	●	●	●	●
Communication, banking, and other facilities	Banking facilities	●	●	●	●	●	●
	Insurance agencies	●	●	◑	○	◑	●
	Restaurants/cafeterias	◑	◑	◑	◑	●	◑
	Overnight lodgings	◑	◑	◑	◑	◑	◑
	Emergency medical facilities	◑	◑	●	◑	●	◑
	Resting areas for drivers	◑	◑	◑	◑	●	◑

BCP = border crossing point.

● At the BCP ◑ In the vicinity of BCP ○ Not applicable/no response

Source: Study team's analysis based on the Cross-Border Trade and Transport Facilitation Index survey responses.

Table 16 presents recommendations for BCPs.

Table 16: Border Crossing Point-Specific Recommendation for Supportive Industrial and Logistic Infrastructure

#	Border Crossing Point	Recommendation
1	**Kirmizi Korpu, Azerbaijan**[a]	• With fresh citrus fruits being one of the top-three cargo commodities passing the BCP, establishing cold storage warehouse near the BCP would be relevant. Fresh fruits are highly perishable and sensitive to temperature fluctuations, and delays caused by customs clearance, document verification, or congestion at the border can compromise their shelf life or result in spoilage. Cold storage facilities at this BCP will help maintain the integrity of the cold chain during transshipment, inspection, or unforeseen wait times, thereby reducing losses and preserving product quality.
2	**Tsiteli Khidi, Georgia**	• Development of product-testing labs and third-party inspection facilities to ensure that the goods meet international quality, safety, and regulatory standards before crossing the border as well as provide independent verification of product quality, weight, and conformity, enhancing trust in trade transactions. • Ensuring availability of material-handling equipment to improve cargo handling efficiency, reducing loading and unloading times, and minimizing damage to goods. • Further, the utilization ratio of Tsiteli Khidi BCP stands quite high at 1.85, wherein the traffic is further expected to increase by 8%–10% in the next few years, necessitating expansion of BCP capacity with higher number of exclusive lanes for truck examination.
3	**Farap, Turkmenistan**	• Provisions for facilities such as availability of insurance agencies may be created in the vicinity of Farap BCP. • Considering Farap BCP's strategic location as a gateway between Turkmenistan and Uzbekistan and Turkmenistan's broader trade facilitation goals, the construction of a logistics hub or dry port at this site may be useful. Such an initiative would bolster regional connectivity, streamline cargo handling, and support the country's aspirations to become a key transit hub in Central Asia.[b]
4	**Yallama, Uzbekistan**	• Yallama BCP may also look at the development of product-testing labs and third-party inspection facilities at the BCP.

BCP = border crossing point.

[a] While the proximity of Baku and Tbilisi provides substantial logistics support to the Kirmizi Korpu–Tsiteli Khidi BCP, the development of a dedicated dry port or a logistics hub at this border could further improve trade efficiency. The Vienna Programme of Action for Landlocked Developing Countries (2014–2024) emphasizes the role of transit countries like Azerbaijan in establishing logistics hubs to promote economies of scale in transport systems and improve border-crossing processes (ADB 2024). Additionally, the Government of Azerbaijan has approved a logistics and trade development road map and undertaken feasibility studies for regional trade and logistics centers (ADB 2023). However, considering the significant investments already made in regional logistics infrastructure, a detailed feasibility study is recommended to evaluate demand, conduct a cost–benefit analysis, and assess potential synergies or overlaps with existing facilities before moving forward with such a development.

[b] Considering the proximity of existing logistics infrastructure in Turkmenabat, which may already serve regional logistics needs, it is suggested that any proposal for a logistics hub or dry port at Farap be subject to a detailed feasibility study. This may include assessing the current and projected cargo volumes, capacity at existing facilities as well as cost–benefit implications.

Source: Study team's suggestions based on the Cross-Border Trade and Transport Facilitation Index analysis.

To bolster regional trade competitiveness and economic development, it is recommended to establish value-added processing centers near key BCPs, such as Torkham in Pakistan. The recent advancements at Torkham, including the near-completion of the Integrated Transit Trade Management System have significantly enhanced trade efficiency, creating an enabling environment for processing centers that can transform raw materials into higher-value products, particularly in sectors like agriculture and textiles. Such initiatives can increase the value-to-weight ratio of exports, reduce transportation costs, and stimulate local employment. Similar assessments may be conducted for other BCPs to evaluate the potential for establishing value-added processing facilities that align with each region's comparative advantages and infrastructure capabilities.

Box 7 showcases how such support facilities have aided the performance of BCPs in the Kyrgyz Republic.

Box 7: Role of Logistic Support Infrastructure in the Kyrgyz Republic

Border Crossing Points in the Kyrgyz Republic

- The time needed to cross the border by road dropped by 24% from 3.7 hours in 2021 to 2.8 hours in 2022. The reduction of outbound road crossing time from 4.7 hours to 2.1 hours was a major factor. This could be attributed to creating a network of cold chain logistics facilities for perishable products that enables the Kyrgyz Republic to stabilize supplies and fetch the best price for agricultural production that is so important to its economy.

- This involves the development of temperature-controlled facilities, a modern refrigerated vehicle fleet, certified testing laboratories, and repair and maintenance centers for refrigerated trucks and containers.

- A training program in cold chain logistics was also an essential part for development. Temperature-controlled facilities and refrigerated trucks are highly capital intensive, and operators must learn how to manage them efficiently to deliver adequate returns.

Sources: ADB 2022c and Refindustry. https://refindustry.com/news/cold-chain/new-cold-storage-facility-opens-in-kyrgyz-republic-s-osh-region/.

Harmonize Transport and Vehicle Standards

Harmonizing transport and vehicle standards for BCPs in CAREC is highly essential for trade facilitation. Successful harmonization requires strong political support, in which CAREC countries need to prioritize transport and vehicle standards within their national agendas and regional cooperation frameworks.

Recommendation 7: Implement standard regulation for supporting border-crossing transit in the CAREC region

The CAREC countries can adopt common technical standards for vehicles, including safety requirements, emissions standards, and vehicle specifications. This would include harmonizing vehicle types, weight limits, axle configurations, and dimensions (UNECE n.d.). The BCPs should establish uniform vehicle inspection procedures to ensure compliance with agreed standards. This would reduce delays at the border points and ensure safety and environmental protection.

CAREC countries may work together to develop a regional agreement/memorandum of understanding that standardizes border transit procedures, including customs documentation, clearance processes, vehicle regulations, transit permits, and vehicular dimensions regulation.

Figure 51 presents the performance of the selected BCPs under limitations for weight and vehicle dimensions.

Figure 51: Performance of Border Crossing Points Under the Weight and Dimension Limitations

	Kirmizi Korpu Azerbaijan	Tsiteli Khidi Georgia	Serhetabat Turkmenistan	Farap Turkmenistan	Torkham Pakistan	Yallama Uzbekistan
Weight limit for cargo vehicles	Present	Present	Absent	Absent	Present	Present
Dimension limitation for cargo vehicles	Present	Present	Absent	Absent	Absent	Present

● Present ○ Absent

Source: Study team's analysis based on the Cross-Border Trade and Transport Facilitation Index survey responses.

All the CAREC countries shall coordinate and regularize the standard weight and dimension limits for trucks and/or containers so that these measures do not become additional checks for customs officials to process the shipments. Box 8 details the European Union's standardized vehicle dimensions.

Box 8: Best Practice Case Study—European Union

European Union (EU)

- The EU has a highly harmonized system for transport and vehicle standards, with common rules and regulations for market access, transport safety, and vehicle technical requirements (including weight, dimension, and axle standards) within its member states.
- The Schengen Borders Code provides EU countries with a single set of common rules that govern external border checks on cargo, entry requirements, and duration of short stays in the Schengen Area.
- In addition, the United Nations Economic Commission for Europe guides harmonizing and simplifying border crossing procedures for inland transport. It has set up World Forum for Harmonization of Vehicle Regulations, a working party to manage the multilateral agreements regulating the technical prescriptions for the construction, approval ofwheeled vehicles and their periodic technical inspection.

Source: European Commission. https://transport.ec.europa.eu/transport-modes/road/non-eu-countries_en.

Way Forward on the Cross-Border Trade and Transport Facilitation Index for Enhancing Policymaking

The CBTTFI developed based on Sub-national Trade Readiness Assessment framework has provided granular information on BCPs to identify possible reasons for delay and higher costs occurring at border crossings. To enhance its effectiveness and relevance in policymaking, the following steps may be incorporated into its framework.

- **Refining the questionnaire**
  The current questionnaire may be expanded to cover a broader range of factors influencing trade and transport facilitation. This includes more detailed questions on infrastructure quality, procedural efficiency and stakeholder engagement.

- **Inclusion of port and rail border crossing points**
  Currently, the CBTTFI focuses on road crossing points only. For a more holistic view, it may be essential to include port and rail crossing points in the assessment. This will help identify bottlenecks and areas for improvement across different modes of transport.

- **Assessment of level of implementation of provisions**
  Questions that assess the level of implementation of trade facilitation measures may be introduced. This includes understanding the extent to which policies and procedures have been adopted and operationalized. Further, data may be collected on the time frame within which implemented systems have been operational. This will help evaluate the effectiveness and sustainability of these measures over time.

- **Harmonized weight and dimension restrictions across border crossing point pairs**
  To enhance the effectiveness of trade facilitation assessments, future analyses may prioritize the harmonization of weight and dimension restrictions across both sides of each BCP pair. While this report adopts the interim assumption that the absence of such restrictions is favorable, it recognizes that misalignment between counterpart BCPs—whether in the presence or thresholds of restrictions—can significantly impede cargo flow, leading to delays, duplicate inspections, or rerouting. Going forward, efforts may focus on collecting and integrating bilateral BCP data, with support from relevant regional stakeholders, to enable a more comprehensive and accurate evaluation. Harmonized restrictions may be treated as a key criterion in cross-border infrastructure planning and policy coordination.

- **Inclusive participation**
  Active participation of all relevant stakeholders, including government agencies and the private sector in the CBTTFI process may be ensured. This will help in capturing diverse perspectives.

- **Site visits and consultative sessions at border crossing points**
  Site visits to selected border crossings are critical for ground-level understanding of operational realities. Holding consultative sessions during these visits is instrumental in presenting preliminary findings, validating responses, and verifying data directly with customs officials and other stakeholders.

This improvement in the CBTTFI framework would enhance the comparative analysis of BCPs regionally and inter-regionally, helping trade analysts and policymakers make informed decisions and formulate guided policies backed by concrete data analysis from the CPMM and the CBTTFI assessment frameworks.

Annex
Questionnaires

Public Sector Questionnaire

Trade Readiness Assessment

A. General Border Crossing Point (BCP) Information

Name of BCP:		
Country:	**Province/Oblast:**	**City:**
CAREC corridor:		
Maximum BCP cargo handling capacity		trucks/containers per day
Expected annual traffic growth rate for next 5 years		% per year
Top-three cargo commodities passing this BCP **1.**	**2.**	**3.**

Traffic through this BCP	Both passenger and freight Freight vehicles only	Yes/No (highlight one) Yes/No (highlight one)				
BCP age	Established in year: Last renovated/upgraded in year:					
Operating hours (use 24-hour format, such as 2000 for 8 p.m.)	Monday	From:	To:	; From:	To:	
	Tuesday	From:	To:	; From:	To:	
	Wednesday	From:	To:	; From:	To:	
	Thursday	From:	To:	; From:	To:	
	Friday	From:	To:	; From:	To:	
	Saturday	From:	To:	; From:	To:	
List all days that the BCP is closed (e.g., important holidays)	Sunday (please note the times the BCP is closed for meals or rest)	From:	To:	; From:	To:	
Operating hours of neighbor country BCP (use 24-hour format, such as 2000 for 8 p.m.).	Monday	From:	To:	; From:	To:	
	Tuesday	From:	To:	; From:	To:	
	Wednesday	From:	To:	; From:	To:	
	Thursday	From:	To:	; From:	To:	
	Friday	From:	To:	; From:	To:	
	Saturday	From:	To:	; From:	To:	
List all days that the neighbor country BCP is closed (e.g., important holidays)	Sunday (please note the times the BCP is closed for meals or rest)	From:	To:	; From:	To:	

continued on next page

Table *continued*

Capacity Estimate the total number of **loaded** trucks using this BCP monthly (import + export + transit)	Average # of trucks		Maximum # of trucks
For import only?			
For export only?			
For transit only?			
Estimate the monthly number of **empty** trucks passing through BCP			
Please highlight the peak months for cross border passage	January April July October	February May August November	March June September December

BCP infrastructure	
Queue capacity for trucks entering BCP	vehicles
Queue capacity for trucks exiting BCP	vehicles
Official truck parking areas	vehicles
Number of lanes of the access roads to this BCP	lanes in each direction
Number of lanes of the connecting road from this BCP to the neighboring country BCP	lanes in each direction
Total no. of mixed-use lanes for both passenger vehicle and truck inspection	lanes
Total no. of lanes used exclusively for truck examination (if applicable)	lanes
No. of green lanes for expedited examination	lanes
No. of regular examination lanes	lanes
No. of red lanes for stringent examination	lanes
How often will the designation of green, regular, red lanes change per month?	times/month
Explain the reasons behind such changes	
No. of drive through large truck scanners	scanners
No. of X-ray scanners for individual shipments	scanners

Name all border management agencies and highlight the sequence of their work in relation to customs inspection. Please add more agencies if not listed in the table.

No.	Name of Agencies	Prior to Customs Inspection	At the Same Time of Customs Inspection	After Customs Inspection	Comments
1	Border security	Yes/No	Yes/No	Yes/No	
2	Immigration	Yes/No	Yes/No	Yes/No	
3	Health	Yes/No	Yes/No	Yes/No	
4	Transport inspectorate	Yes/No	Yes/No	Yes/No	
5	Revenue committee	Yes/No	Yes/No	Yes/No	
6.	Others (specify)				

B. Customs Procedures and Formalities

1. Please specify how each of the following documents is processed at the border office.

(For each document type, please put a √ in relevant columns as applicable)

Document Type	Mandatory Physical Submission of Original Document	Provision to Upload Document in Electronic System Prior to Arrival	Provision to Process Documents Electronically by Customs	Not Applicable
Passport or national ID card				
Visa				
Commercial driver's license				
Permit for vehicle entry				
Vehicle registration document				
Certificate of liability insurance				
Certificate of cargo insurance				
Official weight ticket				
TIR carnet or customs bond				
Bill of lading				
CMR consignment note				
Packing list/cargo manifest				
Customs declaration				
Certificate of origin				
SPS certificate				
Commercial inspection certificate				
Certificate of standard conformance				
Commercial invoice				
Others *(please specify)*				

2. Is ICT infrastructure present at the BCP?

(For each row, please put a √ in relevant columns)

	Presence of Infra	If Present, Please Mention Service Level Up-Time (%)	Not Applicable
Single window portal and relevant applications			
Automated customs management system *(24/7 automated processing of customs declarations)*			
Electronic payment/digital payment of duties and taxes			
Electronic application for customs refunds			
Electronic queue management systems			

continued on next page

Table *continued*

	Presence of Infra	If Present, Please Mention Service Level Up-Time (%)	Not Applicable
Nonintrusive cargo inspection equipment			
Computerized transit control systems			
Automated passport control systems			
Video surveillance systems			
Automatic radiation detection systems			
Portable illegal drug identification systems			
Automated systems for SPS inspection and declarations			
e-TIR			
e-CMR			
Customs mobile app			

3. Are there established procedures for pre-arrival processing?

(Please put a √ in one or more rows as applicable)

	Tick
There is prior intimation on documentation requirements	
There is prior intimation on testing and/or certification requirements	
There is prior intimation of inspection requirement upon risk assessment *(upon submission of pre-arrival information with authorities)*	
There is a provision to make advance fee payment for inspections	
Pre-arrival clearance is given based on submission of requisite documents/information	
Procedures are in place but not practiced	
No such procedures are in place	

4. Is there a system for computerized risk-based assessment for undertaking inspections?

(Please put a √ in relevant row)

	Tick
Yes, physical inspection only takes place based on feedback from computerized risk assessment algorithms	
Officials have overriding/discretionary powers to carry out physical inspections beyond findings of computerized risk assessment algorithms	
No, there is absence of computerized risk-based assessment with 100% physical inspection	

5. What is the percentage of physical inspection?

(Please put a √ in relevant column)

Declaration Type	Less Than 5%	5%–10%	10%–25%	25%–50%	More Than 50% and Less Than 100%
Percentage of physical Inspection *(average percentage in the last 12 months)*					

6. Are there sufficient staff available for undertaking inspections at BCPs?

(Please put a √ in relevant row)

	Tick
Yes, sufficient staff are available for inspections at all times. No delays happen for inspection	
Yes, border control staff are available at all times. However, delays still happen from time to time	
No, insufficient border control staff, frequent delays	

7. Does customs valuation take place based on WTO agreement on customs valuation

(transaction value prescribed by the ACV/customs value code)?

(Please put a √ in relevant row)

	Tick
Yes	
No *(If no, please provide details)*	

8. Is the customs classification consistent among customs headquarters and border branch offices?

(Please put a √ in relevant row)

	Tick
Yes	
No	

C. Customs Coordination

9. Are there any provisions of joint customs control operations?

(Please put a √ in one or more rows as applicable)

	Tick
Interoperable information systems between customs authorities	
Synchronized clearance procedures	
Electronic data interchange between customs authorities	

10. Is there any provision for mutual recognition of documents?
(Please put a √ in one or more rows as applicable)

	Tick
Inspection certificates	
SPS certificates	
AEO certification	
Vehicle registration documents and permits	
Customs guarantee for transport and cargo	
Driver's license	
Insurance documents	
Quality certifications	

D. Support Facilities (within 50 kilometer radius of BCP)

11. What kind of industrial/logistical infrastructure is present at the BCP/in its vicinity?
(For each row, please put a √ in relevant column(s))

	At the BCP	In the Vicinity of BCP	Not Applicable
Hard Infrastructure			
Logistics hub			
Dry ports			
General storage warehouses			
Customs bonded warehouses			
Cold storage warehouses			
Cargo transloading terminals			
Secure vehicle parking lots			
Maintenance-repair facilities for vehicles			
Vehicle fueling stations			
Industrial parks/clusters			
Free trade zones			
Border economic zones			
Certification and Testing Infrastructure			
Product testing laboratories			
Facilities for third-party inspection			
Quarantine treatment centers			
Equipment and Systems			
Material handling equipment for heavy cargo			
Stand-by electric power generators			

continued on next page

Table *continued*

	At the BCP	In the Vicinity of BCP	Not Applicable
Communication, Banking, and Other Facilities			
Banking facilities			
Insurance agencies			
Restaurants or cafeterias			
Overnight lodgings			
Emergency medical facilities			
Resting areas for drivers			
Please provide your inputs on what kind of infrastructure improvements are required at the BCP?			

12. Is internet and mobile connectivity available at the location?

(Please put a √ in relevant column)

Connectivity Type	Yes	No
Mobile connectivity		
Internet connectivity		

E. Transport Regulations

13. Is there any weight limit for cargo vehicles?

(Please put a √ in relevant row)

	Tick
No	
Yes *(If yes, please provide details of weight restrictions)*	

14. Is there any dimension limitation for cargo vehicles?

(Please put a √ in relevant row)

	Tick
No	
Yes *(If yes, please provide details of dimension restrictions)*	

Private Sector Questionnaire

Trade Readiness Assessment

A. General BCP Information

Name of BCP:		
Country:	**Province/Oblast:**	**City:**
CAREC Corridor:		

B. Customs Procedures and Formalities

1. Please specify how each of the following documents is processed at the border office.
(For each document type, please put a √ in relevant columns as applicable)

Document Type	Mandatory Physical Submission of Original Document	Provision to Upload Document in Electronic System Prior to Arrival	Provision to Process Documents Electronically by Customs	Not Applicable
Passport or national ID card				
Visa				
Commercial driver's license				
Permit for vehicle entry				
Vehicle registration document				
Certificate of liability insurance				
Certificate of cargo insurance				
Official weight ticket				
TIR carnet or customs bond				
Bill of lading				
CMR consignment note				
Packing list/cargo manifest				
Customs declaration				
Certificate of origin				
SPS certificate				
Commercial inspection certificate				
Certificate of standard conformance				
Commercial invoice				
Others *(please specify)*				

2. Is ICT infrastructure present at the BCP?

(For each row, please put a √ in relevant columns)

	Presence of Infra	If Present, Please Mention Service Level Up-Time (%)	Not Applicable
Single window portal and relevant applications			
Automated customs management system *(24/7 automated processing of customs declarations)*			
Electronic payment/digital payment of duties and taxes			
Electronic application for customs refunds			
Electronic queue management systems			
Nonintrusive cargo inspection equipment			
Computerized transit control systems			
Automated passport control systems			
Video surveillance systems			
Automatic radiation detection systems			
Portable illegal drug identification systems			
Automated systems for SPS inspection and declarations			
e-TIR			
e-CMR			
Customs mobile app			

3. What steps are taken to enhance border control activities at the BCP?

(Please put a √ in one or more rows as applicable)

	Tick
Single window clearance system is in place, but does not capture all clearances/procedures from partner-government agencies	
Comprehensive single window clearance system is in place	
Authorities undertake joint inspections	
Same documents are required to be shared only once with customs authorities for approvals	
There is no overlap of jurisdiction/powers of officials from different agencies on clearances	
Data sharing with neighboring country's customs	

4. Are there established procedures for pre-arrival processing?
(Please put a √ in one or more rows as applicable)

	Tick
There is prior intimation on documentation requirements	
There is prior intimation on testing and/or certification requirements	
There is prior intimation of inspection requirement upon risk assessment *(upon submission of pre-arrival information with authorities)*	
There is a provision to make advance fee payment for inspections	
Pre-arrival clearance is given based on submission of requisite documents/information	
Procedures are in place but not practiced	
No such procedures are in place	

5. Are there sufficient staff available for undertaking inspections at BCPs?
(Please put a √ in relevant row)

	Tick
Yes, sufficient staff are available for inspections at all times. No delays happen for inspection	
Yes, border control staff are available at all times. However, delays still happen from time to time	
No, insufficient border control staff, frequent delays	

6. Does customs valuation take place based on WTO agreement on customs valuation
(transaction value prescribed by the ACV/customs value code)?
(Please put a √ in relevant row)

	Tick
Yes	
No *(If no, please provide details)*	

7. Do customs officers have sufficient knowledge of various forms and certificates?
(Please put a √ in relevant row)

	Tick
Yes	
No *(If no, please provide specific case examples)*	

8. Is the customs clearance process efficient and expedient?

(Please put a √ in relevant row)

	Tick
Nearly always	
Mostly	
Sometimes	
Rarely	
Hardly ever	
Please provide your inputs on how border control processes can be improved/made more efficient?	

C. Support Facilities (within 50-kilometer radius of BCP)

9. What kind of industrial/logistical infrastructure is present at the border crossing point/in its vicinity?

(For each row, please put a √ in relevant column(s))

	At the BCP	In the Vicinity of BCP	Not Applicable
Hard Infrastructure			
Logistics hub			
Dry ports			
General storage warehouses			
Customs bonded warehouses			
Cold storage warehouses			
Cargo transloading terminals			
Secure vehicle parking lots			
Maintenance-repair facilities for vehicles			
Vehicle fueling stations			
Industrial parks/clusters			
Free trade zones			
Border economic zones			
Certification and Testing Infrastructure			
Product testing laboratories			
Facilities for third-party inspection			
Quarantine treatment centers			
Equipment and Systems			
Material handling equipment for heavy cargo			
Stand-by electric power generators			

continued on next page

Table *continued*

	At the BCP	In the Vicinity of BCP	Not Applicable
Communication, Banking, and Other Facilities			
Banking facilities			
Insurance agencies			
Restaurants or cafeterias			
Overnight lodgings			
Emergency medical facilities			
Resting areas for drivers			
Please provide your inputs on what kind of infrastructure improvements are required at the BCP?			

10. Is Internet and Mobile connectivity available at the location?

(Please put a √ in relevant column)

Connectivity Type	Yes	No
Mobile connectivity		
Internet connectivity		

References

African Union Development Agency (AUDA-NEPAD). 2021. *Enhancing Border Security in Africa Using Smart Border Control Technologies.* https://www.nepad.org/blog/enhancing-border-security-africa-using-smart-border-control-technologies.

Asian Development Bank (ADB). n.d. *Development Asia: Facilitating Cross-Border Trade in Yallama.* https://development.asia/insight/facilitating-cross-border-trade-yallama#:~:text=A%20project%20of%20the%20Government,that%20can%20constrict%20trade%20flow.

———. n.d. *CAREC 2030 Program Results Framework Impact: Sustainable Economic Development and Shared Prosperity for the CAREC Region.* https://www.carecprogram.org/uploads/CAREC-2030-Program-Results-Framework.pdf.

———. 2012. *Trade and Transport Facilitation in the Greater Mekong Subregion.* https://www.greatermekong.org/sites/default/files/trade-and-trade-facilitation-gms.pdf.

———. 2014. *South Asia Subregional Economic Cooperation Trade Facilitation Strategic Framework 2014–2018.* https://www.adb.org/sites/default/files/publication/111017/sasec-tf-strategic-framework-2014-2018.pdf.

———. 2017. *CAREC 2030 Connecting the Region for Shared and Sustainable Development.* https://www.carecprogram.org/uploads/2017-CAREC-2030.pdf.

———. 2019. *CAREC Integrated Trade Agenda 2030 and Rolling Strategic Action Plan 2018–2020.* https://www.adb.org/documents/carec-trade-agenda-2030-action-plan-2018-2020.

———. 2022a. *Progress in Trade Facilitation in CAREC Countries: A 10-Year Corridor Performance Measurement and Monitoring Perspective.* https://www.adb.org/sites/default/files/publication/844686/progress-trade-facilitation-carec-countries.pdf.

———. 2022b. *Integrated Approach to Trade and Transport Facilitation: Measuring Readiness for Sustainable, Inclusive, and Resilient Trade.* https://www.adb.org/sites/default/files/publication/850146/integrated-approach-trade-transport-facilitation.pdf.

———. 2022c. *CAREC Corridor Performance Measurement and Monitoring: Annual Report 2022.* https://cpmm.carecprogram.org/uploads/CAREC-Corridor-Performance-Measurement-Monitoring-Annual-Report-2022.pdf.

———. 2023. *The Developer's Guide to Planning and Designing Logistics Centers in CAREC Countries.* CAREC Program Publication.

———. 2024. Transit Trade Facilitation in Azerbaijan, Kazakhstan and Uzbekistan. Transit Trade Facilitation in Azerbaijan, Kazakhstan, and Uzbekistan | CAREC Program Publication.

Government of Azerbaijan. 2016. Strategic Road Map for Development of Logistics and Trade in the Republic of Azerbaijan. https://monitoring.az/assets/upload/files/4eae769862be45d63dcd5b50b1d31844.pdf.

Organisation for Economic Co-operation and Development (OECD). 2023. *Insights on the Business Climate in Kazakhstan.* OECD Publishing. https://doi.org/10.1787/bd780306-en.

Samad, Ghulam, Amjad Masood, and Junaid Ahmed. 2023. Geographical Proximity and Trade Impacts in the Central Asia Regional Economic Cooperation Program Region. *ADB East Asia Working Paper Series.* No. 60. https://www.adb.org/sites/default/files/publication/870111/eawp-060-geographical-proximity-trade-impacts-carec.pdf.

United Nations Economic and Social Commission for Asia and the Pacific (UNESCAP). n.d. *Handbook on the Requirements for Cross-Border Transport along the Asian Highway Network.* https://www.unescap.org/sites/default/files/English%20version-Handbook-AH%26Indicators-final.pdf.

———. 2014. *Development and Operation of Dry Ports of International Importance.* https://www.unescap.org/sites/default/d8files/event-documents/E_ESCAP_CTR%284%29_3_E.pdf.

———. 2018. *Cross-Border Single Window Interoperability: A Managerial Guide.* https://www.unescap.org/sites/default/files/CROSSBORDER%20SINGLE%20WINDOW%20INTEROPERABILITY.pdf.

———. 2021. *Digital and Sustainable Trade Facilitation in Asia and the Pacific 2021: Based on the United Nations Global Survey on Digital and Sustainable Trade Facilitation.* https://www.unescap.org/sites/default/d8files/knowledge-products/UNTF%20Report.pdf.

———. 2024a. *Pathways to Digital Transformation and Trade Digitalization.* https://www.carecprogram.org/uploads/Session-3.d_Duval.pdf.

———. 2024b. *Advancing Cross-Border Paperless of Mongolia: Reviewing Selected Documents and Exploring Pilot Projects.* https://repository.unescap.org/server/api/core/bitstreams/72570732-98a6-441a-9d8d-efb4ba0707ea/content.

United Nations Economic Commission for Europe (UNECE). n.d. World Forum for Harmonization of Vehicle Regulations (WP.29). https://unece.org/transport/vehicle-regulations/world-forum-harmonization-vehicle-regulations-wp29.

———. 2012. Handbook of Best Practices at Border Crossing – A Trade and Transport Facilitation Perspective. https://unece.org/transport/publications/handbook-best-practices-border-crossing-trade-and-transport-facilitation.

World Bank. 2010. *Trade and Transport Facilitation Assessment: A Practical Toolkit for Country Implementation*. https://www.un.org/ohrlls/sites/www.un.org.ohrlls/files/lldcs_publications/tradetransport_facilitation_assessment_practical_toolkit.pdf.

World Customs Organization (WCO) and World Trade Organization (WTO). n.d. The Role of Advanced Technologies in Cross-Border Trade: A Customs Perspective. https://www.wto.org/english/res_e/booksp_e/wcotech22_e.pdf.

World Trade Organization (WTO). n.d. *Easing the flow of goods across borders – Trade Facilitation Agreement*. https://www.wto.org/english/thewto_e/20y_e/wto_tradefacilitation_e.pdf.

www.ingramcontent.com/pod-product-compliance
Lightning Source LLC
Chambersburg PA
CBHW041756220926
51847CB00014B/220
* 9 7 8 9 2 9 2 7 7 3 8 0 9 *